OETRY
past to present

This book is due for return
the last date stamp

by Anthony Farrell

Heinemann

Contents

821
FAR

Section B: Poets

3

Section C: Writing about Poetry

Introduction

Poetry Past to Present is designed to help you prepare for GCSE English, GCSE English Literature and for Standard Grade. It aims to help you approach poetry with confidence by ensuring that:

◆ you have the skills to respond to poems in a personal and imaginative way

◆ you are able to respond sensitively to the poets' language and to understand why poets choose different forms and styles

◆ you are given lots of practice in comparing poems

◆ you are introduced to a range of poems from different times and different cultures.

Key areas of the new GCSE English and GCSE English Literature syllabuses are covered such as:

◆ pre-twentieth-century poets listed in the National Curriculum and twentieth-century poets with an established critical reputation

◆ poems from other cultures and traditions

◆ poems for comparison.

The book is divided into three sections.

Section A offers a range of different ways to approach poems, introduces you to some poetic forms and literary terms and develops your skills in comparing poems.

Section B contains poems by seven major poets enabling you to focus on a range of poems by one or more poets for coursework assignments.

Section C is a practical guide to writing about poetry in examinations and in coursework.

While *Poetry Past to Present* clearly focuses on preparing for your exams I hope you will find it is more than an examination book. I hope you enjoy reading the poems selected here and that the memory of some of them will linger long after you have finished your examination course.

Anthony Farrell

A1 *First Responses*

When you read a poem for the first time you shouldn't worry about trying to understand everything in it. You need to read a poem several times and let it work on you. You may find that your response to the poem changes with each reading.

Getting Started

Read this poem by Michael Baldwin then re-read it or listen to it being read aloud. As you read, jot down your responses to the poem. At this point don't worry too much about small details or anything you don't understand.

Death on a Live Wire

Treading a field I saw afar
A laughing fellow climbing the cage
That held the grinning tensions of wire,
Alone, and no girl gave him courage.

5 Up he climbed on the diamond struts.
Diamond cut diamond, till he stood
With the insulators brooding like owls
And all their live wisdom, if he would.

I called to him climbing and asked him to say
10 what thrust him into the singeing sky:
The one word he told me the wind took away,
So I shouted again, but the wind passed me by

And the gust of his answer tore at his coat
And struck him stark on the lightning's bough:
15 Humanity screeched in his manacled throat
And he cracked with flame like a figure of straw.

Turning, burning, he dangled black,
A hot sun swallowing at his fork
And shaking embers out of his back,
20 Planting his shadow of fear in the chalk.

O then he danced an incredible dance
With soot in his sockets, hanging at heels;
Uprooted mandrakes screamed in his loins,
His legs thrashed and lashed like electric eels;

25 For now he embraced the talent of iron,
The white-hot ore that comes from the hill,
The Word out of which the electrons run,
The snake in the rod and the miracle;

And as he embraced it the girders turned black,
30 Fused metal wept and great tears ran down,
Till his fingers like snails at last came unstuck
And he fell through the cage of the sun.

Michael Baldwin

Asking Questions

Asking questions is a simple and well-tried way of getting to grips with a poem. You can ask questions at several different levels.

Level 1

During your first or second reading of the poem ask yourself general questions such as:

◆ what does the title suggest the poem will be about?

◆ does anything in the poem surprise me?

◆ which parts of the poem are puzzling or make me wonder what is going on?

◆ are any words, phrases or images particularly striking?

Make a note of the parts of the poem you think you need to know more about.

Level 2

Read the poem again and this time ask more detailed questions and make detailed notes line by line. You will find it useful to have a copy of the poem to annotate.

sounds dramatic – like a trapeze artist in a circus

Death on a Live Wire

why laughing? is he mad?

Treading a field I saw afar
A laughing fellow climbing the cage ——— *so it's a pylon in a field*
That held the grinning tensions of wire,
why grinning? Alone, and no girl gave him courage.

Activity

1 Make notes asking questions about 'Death on a Live Wire'.

2 Exchange your notes with a partner.

3 On page 157 you will find a copy of this poem which has already been annotated by a Year 11 student. Compare this student's responses with your own.

◆ Have you been drawn to comment on the same lines or phrases?

◆ Did you experience similar feelings?

◆ Did you ask similar questions about aspects of the poem you are unsure about?

A2 Shared Responses

Sharing your views and opinions with other students helps you to deepen your understanding of a poem and to clarify issues which might be raised when you read the poem yourself.

Read this poem by Mary Dorcey and make your own notes about it.

First Love

You were tall and beautiful.
You wore your long brown hair
wound about your head,
your neck stood clear and full
5 as the stem of a vase.
You held my hand in yours
and we walked slowly, talking
of small familiar happenings
and of the lost secrets of
10 your childhood. It seems it was

Always autumn then.
The amber trees shook. We laughed
in a wind that cracked the leaves
from black boughs and set them scuffling
15 about our feet, for me to trample still
and kick in orange clouds
about your face. We would climb dizzy
to the cliff's edge and stare down
at a green and purple sea, the

20 Wind howling in our ears, as it
tore the breath from white cheeked waves.
You steadied me against
the wheeling screech of gulls, and I

loved to think that but for your strength
25 I would tumble to the rocks below
to the fated death, your stories made me
dream of. I don't remember
that I looked in your eyes or that we
ever asked an open question. Our thoughts

30 Passed through our blood, it seemed,
and the slightest pressure of our hands
decided all issues wordlessly.
We watched in silence by the shore
the cold spray against our skin,
35 in mutual need of the water's fierce,
inhuman company, that gave promise
of some future, timeless refuge from
all the fixed anxieties of our world.
As we made for home

40 We faced into the wind, my thighs
were grazed by its icy teeth, you
gathered your coat about me and I
hurried our steps towards home, fire
and the comfort of your sweet, strong tea.
45 We moved bound in step.
You sang me songs of Ireland's sorrows
and of proud women, loved and lost.
I knew them, they set for me
a brilliant stage of characters, who

50 Even now, can seem more real
than my most intimate friends.
We walked together, hand in hand.
You were tall and beautiful,
you wore your long brown hair wound
55 about your head, your neck stood
clear and full as the stem of a vase.
I was young – you were my mother
and it seems, it was always
autumn then.

Mary Dorcey

Activity 1

When you have read the poem yourself, form a group with four or five other students and discuss the poem in detail.

Use these prompts to help you.

◆ What does the title suggest the poem will be about?

◆ Why are phrases from the first verse repeated in the last verse?

◆ Is there any significance in the way in which the poem is divided up into verses? (Think about the content of each verse.)

◆ Were you surprised by the last verse and can you explain why?

◆ Are there any repeated lines or phrases in the poem and, if so, why do you think they have been repeated?

◆ What do you find most memorable or striking about the poem?

Activity 2

Read 'Ain't I A Woman?' on page 12 carefully and make your own personal response to it in note form.

Reading

Choose one or two people in your group to read the poem aloud. Before they read it discuss the following points.

◆ What **tone** would you use to read this poem?
(**Tone** means the *mood* of the poem, e.g. happy, sad, angry, depressed, spirited.)

◆ Are there any particular words or phrases you would emphasize in your reading?

◆ How would you **pace** your reading of the poem? (Would you read it quickly or slowly? Where would you pause?)

◆ Would you read loudly or softly or vary the volume?

If you would like to know more about preparing to read a poem aloud look at Performing Poetry, page 16.

Ain't I A Woman?

That man over there say
    A woman needs to be helped into carriages
and lifted over ditches
    and to have the best place everywhere.
5 Nobody ever helped me into carriages
    or over mud puddles
    or give me a best place . . .
And ain't I a woman?

    Look at me
10 Look at my arm!
    I have plowed and planted
and gathered into barns
    and no man could head me . . .
And ain't I a woman?
15   I could work as much
and eat as much as a man –
    when I could get it –

and bear the lash as well
    and ain't I a woman?
20 I have born 13 children
    and seen most all sold into slavery
and when I cried out a mother's grief
    none but Jesus heard me . . .
and ain't I a woman?
25   that little man in black there say
a woman can't have as much rights as a man
    cause Christ wasn't a woman
Where did your Christ come from?
    From God and a woman!
30 Man had nothing to do with him!
    If the first woman God ever made
was strong enough to turn the world
    upside down, all alone
together women ought to be able to turn it
35   rightside up again.

Sojourner Truth

Statements

1 Consider these six statements carefully and decide whether you agree with them or not. Jot down some notes on your opinions to support your views.

♦ This poem is an attack on traditional Christian values.

♦ Sojourner Truth is simply annoyed because a man would not carry her luggage.

♦ This is a poem written in anger.

♦ Sojourner Truth feels she has been lucky all her life.

♦ Sojourner Truth is bitter because she has had a hard life.

♦ Sojourner Truth is proud of being a woman.

2 In your groups discuss these statements and see whether or not you can reach agreement about them.

Try to explain and support your views by referring closely to the text.

As your discussion progresses you may find yourselves talking about other issues in the poem that interest you.

Activity 3

Read this poem by the Northern Irish poet, Paul Muldoon.

Why Brownlee Left _____

Why Brownlee left, and where he went,
Is a mystery even now.
For if a man should have been content
It was him; two acres of barley,
5 One of potatoes, four bullocks,
A milker, a slated farmhouse.
He was last seen going out to plough
On a March morning, bright and early.

By noon Brownlee was famous;
10 They had found all abandoned, with
The last rig unbroken, his pair of black
Horses, like man and wife,
Shifting their weight from foot to
Foot, and gazing into the future.

Paul Muldoon

13

Statements

1 In groups consider these six statements about 'Why Brownlee Left' and decide whether you agree or disagree with each one. Make notes to support your views.

◆ Brownlee is a farmer.

◆ Brownlee had no obvious reason for running away.

◆ The shock of Brownlee's disappearance was made worse because he was so famous.

◆ Brownlee took his horses with him.

◆ The poet is saying the life of a country farmer is very pleasant.

◆ The poet is suggesting Brownlee's life was boring.

Share your views with other groups.

Writing

The following tasks will help you to reflect more deeply upon the story behind the poem.

1 Write a newspaper article that describes Brownlee's disappearance and suggests reasons for it.

2 Imagine you are a close relative of Brownlee and write a letter to a friend describing events and your feelings about them.

3 Imagine you are Brownlee. Write a short story which explains why you disappeared and where you went.

Activity 4

Look at the following poem by Elizabeth Jennings.

My Grandmother _____

She kept an antique shop – or it kept her.
Among Apostle spoons and Bristol glass,
The faded silks, the heavy furniture,
She watched her own reflection in the brass
5 Salvers and silver bowls, as if to prove
Polish was all, there was no need of love.

And I remember how I once refused
To go out with her, since I was afraid.
It was perhaps a wish not to be used
10 Like antique objects. Though she never said
That she was hurt, I still could feel the guilt
Of that refusal, guessing how she felt.

Later, too frail to keep a shop, she put
All her best things in one long narrow room.
15 The place smelt old, of things too long kept shut,
The smell of absences where shadows come
That can't be polished. There was nothing then
To give her own reflection back again.

And when she died I felt no grief at all,
20 Only the guilt of what I once refused.
I walked into her room among the tall
Sideboards and cupboards – things she never used
But needed: and no finger-marks were there,
Only the new dust falling through the air.

Elizabeth Jennings

Responding

What emotion, do you think, prompted Elizabeth Jennings to write this
poem? Which details in the poem suggest this?

Making your own statements

1 Work with a partner to construct eight statements about this poem,
   some of which you believe to be true and some false.

2 When you have written your statements organize them into a
   worksheet for another group of students to discuss and work on.

You may make similar worksheets based on statements about a poem,
using other poems in this book.

A2 Shared Responses

$A3$ *Performing Poetry*

Many poets believe that the vitality of poetry can only be experienced when poetry is read, or performed live. Reading aloud also helps you to think about the tone (mood) and pace of the poem.

Activity

You are going to prepare a group reading of the poem below. The poem is a dialogue between three people with a narrator describing events. Read the poem carefully and identify which character speaks each piece of dialogue.

The Fear

A lantern light from deeper in the barn
Shone on a man and woman in the door
And threw their lurching shadows on a house
Nearby, all dark in every glossy window.
5   A horse's hoof pawed once the hollow floor,
And the back of the gig they stood beside
Moved in a little. The man grasped a wheel,
The woman spoke out sharply, 'Whoa, stand still!
I saw it just as plain as a white plate,'
10   She said, 'as the light on the dashboard ran
Along the bushes at the roadside – a man's face.
You *must* have seen it too.'

'I didn't see it.

Are you sure –'

15   'Yes, I'm sure!'

                '– it was a face?'

'Joel, I'll have to look. I can't go in,
I can't, and leave a thing like that unsettled.
Doors locked and curtains drawn will make no
20   difference.
I always have felt strange when we came home
To the dark house after so long an absence,
And the key rattled loudly into place
Seemed to warn someone to be getting out
25 At one door as we entered at another.
What if I'm right, and someone all the time –
Don't hold my arm!'
                              'I say it's someone passing.'

'You speak as if this were a travelled road.
30 You forget where we are. What is beyond
That he'd be going to or coming from
At such an hour of night, and on foot too?
What was he standing still for in the bushes?'

'It's not so very late – it's only dark.
35 There's more in it than you're inclined to say.
Did he look like – ?'

'He looked like anyone.
I'll never rest tonight unless I know.
Give me the lantern.'

40   'You don't want the lantern.'

She pushed past him and got it for herself.

'You're not to come,' she said. 'This is my business.
If the time's come to face it, I'm the one
To put it the right way. He'd never dare –
45 Listen! He kicked a stone. Hear that, hear that!
He's coming towards us. Joel, go in – please.
Hark! – I don't hear him now. But please go in.'

'In the first place you can't make me believe it's – '

'It is – or someone else he's sent to watch.
50 And now's the time to have it out with him
While we know definitely where he is.
Let him get off and he'll be everywhere
Around us, looking out of trees and bushes
Till I shan't dare to set a foot outdoors.
55 And I can't stand it. Joel, let me go!'

'But it's nonsense to think he'd care enough.'

'You mean you couldn't understand his caring.
Oh, but you see he hadn't had enough –
Joel, I won't – I won't – I promise you.
60 We mustn't say hard things. You mustn't either.'

'I'll be the one, if anybody goes!
But you give him the advantage with this light.
What couldn't he do to us standing here!
And if to see was what he wanted, why,
65 He has seen all there was to see and gone.'

He appeared to forget to keep his hold,
But advanced with her as she crossed the grass.

'What do you want?' she cried to all the dark.
She stretched up tall to overlook the light
70 That hung in both hands, hot against her skirt.

'There's no one; so you're wrong,' he said.
                                    'There is. –
What do you want?' she cried, and then herself
Was startled when an answer really came.

75 'Nothing.' It came from well along the road.

She reached a hand to Joel for support:

The smell of scorching woollen made her faint.
'What are you doing round this house at night?'

'Nothing.' A pause: there seemed no more to say.

80 And then the voice again: 'You seem afraid.
I saw by the way you whipped up the horse.
I'll just come forward in the lantern light
And let you see.'

                    'Yes, do. – Joel, go back!'

85 She stood her ground against the noisy steps
That came on, but her body rocked a little.

'You see,' the voice said.

                        'Oh.' She looked and looked.

'You don't see – I've a child here by the hand.
90 A robber wouldn't have his family with him.'

'What's a child doing at this time of night – ?'
'Out walking. Every child should have the memory
Of at least one long-after-bedtime walk.
What, son?'

95 'Then I should think you'd try to find
Somewhere to walk –'

                        'The highway, as it happens –
We're stopping for a fortnight down at Dean's.'

'But if that's all – Joel – you realize –
100 You won't think anything. You understand?
You understand that we have to be careful.
This is a very, very lonely place. –
Joel!' She spoke as if she couldn't turn.
The swinging lantern lengthened to the ground,
105 It touched, it struck, it clattered and went out.

Robert Frost

Group reading

Work in a group with three other people to prepare a dramatic reading of this poem.

◆ Annotate a copy of the poem to highlight your reading part.
◆ Look at the punctuation carefully. It is there to help you make an accurate reading of the poem.
◆ Decide how to deliver your part.

You will need to consider:

◆ the **pace** of the poem (it may vary in different parts of the poem): slow, brisk, rapid and so on
◆ the **tone** of voice required: threatening, calm, scared, questioning and so on
◆ the amount of dramatic emphasis necessary: loud, passionate, subdued
◆ the emotions to be conveyed: anger, fear, suspicion
◆ the value of pauses.

When annotating the poem for your reading, you may find these letters or symbols helpful:

/	means pause briefly
//	means a longer pause
p	means speak softly
f	means speak loudly or with emphasis.

Rehearse your reading carefully and then perform it live or tape it.

Discussion

When you have performed the poem, speculate about the situation it describes and discuss it with your group.

Writing

◆ Write about what happens after the lantern strikes the ground, using prose, not poetry.
◆ In groups, prepare short dramatic sketches which explain events leading up to the incident described in the poem.

A4 *Looking at Language*

When you're discussing poetry, reading about it or being asked to write about it, you will come across various specialist words known as **literary terms**. You will find it helpful to be able to use these terms as they often make it easier to say what you want clearly. This unit revises literary terms you may have already met.

Be careful not to use literary terms in your essays just for the sake of using them. You won't gain good marks if all you do is give a list of the images in a poem. It's only worthwhile using these special terms if they help you to say something about the meaning of the poem or about your response to it.

Imagery

We use imagery to make our meanings more dramatic and interesting. Images are pictures created through words. They're often created by comparing one thing with something else.

Visual imagery appeals to our sense of sight and creates pictures in our minds, for example:

> Dawn breaks open like a wound that bleeds afresh.

This very short poem by Amy Lowell creates a single, striking visual image.

Peace

Perched upon the muzzle of a cannon
A yellow butterfly is slowly opening and shutting its wings.

Amy Lowell

Aural imagery appeals to our sense of hearing. In the type of aural imagery known as **onomatopoeia** the sound of a word echoes its meaning. Writers sometimes use onomatopeia to create a sense of urgency or tension, for instance:

> The shrill, demented choirs of wailing shells

from Wilfred Owen's 'Anthem for Doomed Youth' or, from Coleridge's 'The Rime of the Ancient Mariner':

> The ice was here, the ice was there,
> The ice was all around:
> It cracked and growled, and roared and howled,
> Like noises in a swound!

Writers also use repeated sound patterns at the beginning of words. This is known as **alliteration**.

The repeated sounds in this stanza, also from 'The Rime of the Ancient Mariner,' suggest the flowing motion of the ship:

> Swiftly, swiftly flew the ship,
> Yet she sailed softly too:
> Sweetly, sweetly blew the breeze –
> On me alone it blew.

This short extract of Old English poetry comes from 'The Battle of Maldon' (fought in 991) when the English Lord Byrhtnoth is fighting for his life against a band of Viking raiders. Notice the emphasis of 'b' sounds which reinforces the sense of the brutality of battle.

> Þā Byrhtnoð brād bill of scēaðe
>
> brād and brūnecg, and on þā byrnan slōh

(Then Byrhtnoth drew his broad and bright-edged sword from its sheath and smote upon his [the Viking's] breastplate.)

Images may also appeal to other senses such as touch, taste and smell.

Activity 1

Below are two verses from a poem by T. S. Eliot. The poem is rich in images which are skilfully used to work on our different senses.

Preludes _____

I

    The winter evening settles down
    With smell of steaks in passageways.
    Six o'clock.
    The burnt-out ends of smoky days.
5 And now a gusty shower wraps
    The grimy scraps
    Of withered leaves about your feet
    And newspapers from vacant lots;
    The showers beat
10 On broken blinds and chimney-pots,
    And at the corner of the street
    A lonely cab-horse steams and stamps.
    And then the lighting of the lamps.

II

    The morning comes to consciousness
15 Of faint stale smells of beer
    From the sawdust-trampled street
    With all its muddy feet that press
    To early coffee-stands.

With the other masquerades
20 That time resumes,
One thinks of all the hands
That are raising dingy shades
In a thousand furnished rooms.

T. S. Eliot

1 In pairs make a list of the images in this poem. Use a chart like the one below and list the images in column 1.

2 Decide which sense the image works on and complete column 2. An image may work on more than one sense.

3 How does the image make you feel? What does it make you think about? What do you associate with the image? Write the *effect* the image has in column 3. Include responses from both you and your partner.

4 Write a paragraph to describe the mood created by the images in this poem.

1 Image	2 Sense	3 Effect
The winter evening settles down		

Similes, metaphors and personification

Similes, metaphors and personification are types of images. They are also known as figures of speech.

Simile

A **simile** is a figure of speech in which an explicit comparison is made between two things which are quite different in kind or quality. The comparison is usually introduced by 'like' or 'as'. For example:

> *It is as dark as night.*

> *They are like two peas in a pod.*

Or, from 'Sowing' by Edward Thomas:

> It was a perfect day
> For sowing; just
> As sweet and dry was the ground
> As tobacco-dust.

Metaphor

Like a simile, a **metaphor** compares one thing with another. Unlike a simile, a metaphor does not use 'like' or 'as' . It describes one thing as though it literally *is* another thing, so the comparison can seem both more subtle than the simile and more powerful.

For example, in this phrase:

> *the motorcar was purring at the red light*

the car is described as a cat. We use metaphors all the time to strengthen our everyday speech.

> *I've been battling all night to finish my English essay.*

Verbs are often used metaphorically in order to strengthen a statement or description:

> *The kettle **sang** on the stove.*

> *The wind **roared** through the trees.*

Metaphors are often very strong images designed to surprise or shock us.

Activity 1

Look at this poem by Phoebe Hesketh.

Geriatric Ward

Feeding time in the geriatric ward;
I wondered how they found their mouths,
and seeing that not one looked up, inquired
'Do they have souls?'

5 'If I had a machine gun,' answered the doctor
'I'd show you dignity in death instead of living death.
Death wasn't meant to be kept alive.
But we're under orders
to pump blood and air in after the mind's gone.
10 I don't understand souls;
I only learned about cells
law-abiding as leaves
withering under frost.
But we, never handing over
15 to Mother who knows best,
spray cabbages with oxygen, hoping for a smile,
count pulses of breathing bags whose direction is lost,
and think we've won.

Here's a game you can't win –
20 One by one they ooze away in the cold.
There's no society forbidding
this dragged-out detention of the old.'

Phoebe Hesketh

Responding

1 What does the doctor think should be allowed to happen to the old people?

   What is your response to this?

2 Identify the metaphors. Do you find them shocking or surprising? Why?

   Write a short paragraph showing how the metaphors reinforce the meaning of the poem.

Extended metaphors

In an **extended metaphor** the comparison is continued for some time in order to extend and deepen the description.

This poem by D. H. Lawrence creates a vivid picture of newly-built suburban houses by using an extended metaphor.

Flat Suburbs, S.W., in the Morning _____

The new red houses spring like plants
    In level rows

Of reddish herbage that bristles and slants
    Its square shadows.

5 The pink young houses show one side bright
    Flatly assuming the sun,
And one side shadow, half in sight.
    Half-hiding the pavement-run;

Where hastening creatures pass intent
10   On their level way,
Threading like ants that can never relent
    And have nothing to say.

Bare stems of street lamps stiffly stand
    At random, desolate twigs,
15 To testify to a blight on the land
    That has stripped their sprigs.

D. H. Lawrence

Responding

◆ What image and comparison is used in this metaphor?

◆ Can you explain why the metaphor used in this extract is so effective? How well does it reinforce the description of new suburban development?

◆ How does D. H. Lawrence use the metaphor to convey his personal feelings about the suburban landscape?

Activity 2

Read this poem by Andrew Young.

Thistledown _____

Silver against blue sky
These ghosts of day float by,
Fitful, irregular,
Each one a silk-haired star,
5 Till from the wind's aid freed
They settle on their seed.

Not by the famished light
Of a moon-ridden night
But by clear sunny hours
10 Gaily these ghosts of flowers
With rise and swirl and fall
Dance to their burial.

Andrew Young

Responding

The essential characteristics of thistledown are seen as ghostly images in this poem.

◆ What is the link between thistledown and ghostly apparitions?
◆ In what sense can thistledown be called the 'ghosts of flowers'?
◆ How effective is this extended metaphor?

Creating metaphors

1   Choose one of these categories:
   ◆ plants
   ◆ cars.

2   Make a list of types you could include in your category, for example:

Plants	Cars
Oak tree	Ford Escort
Bramble	Nissan Primera

3   Suggest a metaphor for each type you have listed. Explain the reason for your choice – for example:

Plant   **Metaphor**

Oak tree   Medieval castle
(both are strong and long-lasting, they are both very English)

Bramble   Barbed wire
(they are similar in appearance and can entangle things, often found on waste ground)

Group work

In a group with two or three other people, think of a person the rest of your class would know (teacher, sports personality, pop star and so on).

Write a description of the mystery personality without naming the person. Using the idea of a simile or extended metaphor, describe your celebrity as if he or she were:

◆ a piece of furniture
◆ a month of the year
◆ an animal
◆ a type of flower
◆ a particular kind of weather.

When you have completed your description, read it to the rest of your class and ask them to guess who it is. You may think of many more areas of comparison. You could try to write them out in verse form.

Personification

Personification takes an inanimate object or an abstract idea and treats it as if it is a person or has human characteristics.

The following poem by T. E. Hulme uses personification to make an autumn evening feel homely and familiar.

Autumn

A touch of cold in the Autumn night –
I walked abroad,
And saw the ruddy moon lean over a hedge
Like a red-faced farmer.
I did not stop to speak, but nodded,
And round about were the wistful stars
With white faces like town children.

T. E. Hulme

Responding

◆ What kind of 'personality' does the poet give to the moon?
◆ What characteristics are given to the stars?
◆ Why do you think the poet sees the moon and the stars as so different?
◆ What is your overall impression of the autumn night?

Now look at this poem by Sylvia Plath.

Mushrooms

Overnight, very
Whitely, discreetly,
Very quietly

Our toes, our noses
5 Take hold on the loam,
Acquire the air.

Nobody sees us,
Stops us, betrays us;
The small grains make room.

10 Soft fists insist on
Heaving the needles,
The leafy bedding,

Even the paving.
Our hammers, our rams,
15 Earless and eyeless,

Perfectly voiceless,
Widen the crannies,
Shoulder through holes. We

Diet on water,
20 On crumbs of shadow,
Bland-mannered, asking

Little or nothing.
So many of us!
So many of us!

25 We are shelves, we are
Tables, we are meek,
We are edible,

Nudgers and shovers
In spite of ourselves.
30 Our kind multiplies:

We shall by morning
Inherit the earth.
Our foot's in the door.

Sylvia Plath

Responding

Read the poem through carefully, and then make a list of all the human characteristics Sylvia Plath has given to mushrooms. Use two separate columns, one headed **Physical characteristics** (e.g. 'soft fists insist . . .') and the other **Behaviour characteristics** (e.g. 'we are meek').

Imaginative response

Write a story, or a poem, in which two non-human objects are in competition with each other. Give them human characteristics and invent a contest for them to participate in. For example, *summer* versus *winter,* or *fire* versus *water.* The contest could be in the form of a race or a wrestling match.

A5 *Looking at Form and Structure*

Form

When people talk about the **form** of a poem they usually mean its shape or pattern.

◆ How is the poem set out on the page?

◆ Does it have long or short lines or a mixture?

◆ Is it divided into verses? If so, do the verses have the same pattern? Do they have the same rhyme scheme?

Activity

In the **shape** poems below, the form clearly mirrors the content.

Mirror _____

When you look	kool uoy nehW
into a mirror	rorrim a otni
it is not	ton si ti
yourself you see,	,ees uoy flesruoy
but a kind	dnik a tub
of apish error	rorre hsipa fo
posed in fearful	lufraef ni desop
symmetry	yrtemmys

John Updike

40–Love _____

middle	aged
couple	playing
ten	nis
when	the
game	ends
and	they
go	home
the	net
will	still
be	be
tween	them

Roger McGough

Responding

These two poems have been treated in the same way on the page, but the reason for their shape and layout is different in each case. Explain why you think each poem is set out the way it is.

Poem About the Sun Slinking Off and Pinning up a Notice _____

```
     the sun
     hasn't got me fooled
     not for a minute
     just when
 5   you're beginning to believe
     that        grass is green
     and         skies are blue
     and         colour is king
     hey         ding a ding ding
10   and
           a
                 host
                     of
                           other
15                              golden
                                    etceteras
     before you know where you are
     he's slunk off somewhere
     and pinned up a notice saying:
20      MOON
```

Roger McGough

Responding

Explain the reason for this poem's rather unusual appearance. How effective is it?

Writing

Compile an anthology of shape poetry. Write some yourself and collect examples from fellow students and from other poetry anthologies.

When writing your own, concentrate on well-known objects with a clear, definite shape or with recognizable characteristics such as a cup, weigh scales, a rocket, a twist drill, a candle and so on.

How is it organized?

When people talk about the **structure** of a poem they're talking about the way it is organized. There are a number of questions you can ask about structure.

◆ Is there a story or plot running through the poem? If so, does the story start at the beginning of the poem and finish at the end?

◆ Does the poem concentrate on a single incident or idea or on lots of images and ideas?

The best way to work out how a poem is structured is to think about what is happening or what the poet is saying in each verse.

Activity 1

This poem, 'The Fight' by Ted Walker, is written in regular four-line verses and has a simple plot. It has a **chronological structure** which means the poem follows the development of a story. The order of the verses has been deliberately jumbled here, however, so the chronological structure has been muddled. Before you read the poem, look at **What to do** on page 36.

The Fight _____

1   Where, in the adjacent graveyard,
    Two pilots lie under the snow.
    I wonder if Michael or I might have won:
    But that's something that we'll never know.

2   We circled each other, like panthers
    (Out of range of each other, of course);
    We glared at each other like tigers,
    Observed by the greengrocer's horse.

3   They spat at each other with bullets;
    When two of them fell in their flames
    Miss Bee led us all to the shelters
    To play mental arithmetic games.

4   Sometimes I see Michael Saunders
    In the pub of a Saturday night.
    Forty years have elapsed since that morning
    When two little boys had a fight:

5   At playtime, quite close to the railings,
    Out of sight from our teacher, Miss Bee,
    I threatened that awful boy, Saunders,
    And he in his turn threatened me.

6   We play cards in the cosy bar-parlour,
    Our glasses of beer side by side;
    In the grate a brisk log-fire is burning;
    We forget that it's winter outside

7   Overhead, the Battle of Britain
    Was beginning in earnest once more;
    Like tigers and panthers, the aircraft
    Were trying to settle the score.

8   I remember, when we were just nippers,
    Michael Saunders and I were sworn foes;
    One morning of sunlit September
    It looked as though we'd come to blows.

9   But Michael still often reminds me
    Of that day. What he always says is:
    'I bet you my Dad could beat your Dad.'
    And I tell him that mine could beat his.

10 He said that he'd tear me to ribbons.
    'You and whose army?' I said.
    (We were terribly witty in those days.)
    I told him I'd kick in his head.

11 Someone pushed me towards Michael Saunders;
    Thank God, he stepped out of the way.
    We started to take off our jackets . . .
    A Spitfire, it was, saved the day.

12 A little crowd gathered around us;
    They egged us both on to begin.
    Kathy Woodward (who wetted her knickers)
    Said she'd notify our next-of-kin.

Ted Walker

A5 Looking at Form and Structure

What to do

1 Working by yourself, reorganize the verses so that they read in the correct order. As well as relying upon the chronological structure of the poem, look out for any other clues you can find.

2 When you have completed the task, compare your version with that of a partner. Are they the same? See if you can reach an agreed reconstruction between you.

3 Now compare your version with the correct form of this poem which can be found on page 155.

Imaginative response

Imagine you had the opportunity to listen to Michael Saunders and Ted Walker talking to each other in the pub one night. Rewrite the conversation in which they capture childhood memories and relive the day of 'The Fight'.

Activity 2

To work out the structure of a poem that doesn't have verses, see if you can break it into sections. For example, you might break the first part of this poem by Edward Thomas into sections as shown.

As the Team's Head-Brass _____

As the team's head-brass flashed out on the turn
The lovers disappeared into the wood. ⎯⎯⎯⎯ watching lovers
disappearing

narrator describes ⎯⎯ I sat among the boughs of the fallen elm
where he is sitting   That strewed an angle of the fallow, and

5 Watched the plough narrowing a yellow square
Of charlock. Every time the horses turned ⎯⎯ focusing
narrator describes   Instead of treading me down, the ploughman leaned   on the
what he can see   Upon the handles to say or ask a word,   ploughman
About the weather, next about the war.

10 Scraping the share he faced towards the wood,
And screwed along the furrow till the brass flashed
Once more.
    The blizzard felled the elm whose crest
I sat in, by a woodpecker's round hole,

15 The ploughman said. 'When will they take it away?'
'When the war's over.' So the talk began –

One minute more and an interval of ten,
A minute more and the same interval.
'Have you been out?' 'No.' 'And don't want to, perhaps?'
20 'If I could only come back again, I should.
I could spare an arm. I shouldn't want to lose
A leg. If I should lose my head, why, so,
I should want nothing more ... . Have many gone
From here?' 'Yes.' 'Many lost?' 'Yes, a good few.
25 Only two teams work on the farm this year.
One of my mates is dead. The second day
In France they killed him. It was back in March,
The very night of the blizzard, too. Now if
He had stayed here we should have moved the tree.'
30 'And I should have not have sat here. Everything
Would have been different. For it would have been
Another world.' 'Ay, and a better, though
If we could see all all might seem good.' Then
The lovers came out of the wood again:
35 The horses started and for the last time
I watched the clods crumble and topple over
After the ploughshare and the stumbling team.

Edward Thomas

Responding

This poem was written in 1916, in the middle of the First World War.
Edward Thomas himself was a soldier in this war and was killed a few
weeks before the war ended.

1 From line 15 onwards work out who is speaking at each point. What
   is the ploughman's attitude to the war?

2 See if you can divide the rest of the poem into
   sections.

3 Why do you think Edward Thomas
   reintroduced the image of the lovers at the end
   of the poem?

   In what ways might the image of the lovers be
   connected with the plough-team and the war?

   Share your suggestions with other members of
   your class and see what points you agree on and
   where you differ.

A5 Looking at Form and Structure

Poetic forms

Some poems conform closely to a definite and recognizable structure and many of these have specific names. Examples of some of these poetic forms are **ballads**, **sonnets**, **haiku**, **odes** and **elegies**.

Poems which have no definite verse pattern or rhyme scheme are said to be written in **free verse**.

In this section we look specifically at the ballad and at sonnets.

The ballad

Traditionally, a **ballad** is a song that tells a story. The story often has a tragic theme or a sad ending. Many ballads date back to the Middle Ages and they were originally passed on from person to person as oral – spoken – literature.

Most ballads have a simple, chronological structure (the events are related in the order in which they happened) organized in plain, four-line **stanzas**. Ballads often tell only one small part of what must originally have been a much larger story. Ballads rarely explain why things happen, they tend only to tell the events. Many ballads present characters speaking in dramatic situations and this adds a lively quality to them. Some ballads exist in a number of different forms and with different titles.

Ballads which date back to the Middle Ages are known as **traditional ballads**, and they are relatively simple poems. Some ballads exist in dialect form which can be more difficult to read.

Literary ballads were developed during the eighteenth and nineteenth centuries by poets such as William Wordsworth, Samuel Coleridge and John Keats. Unlike traditional ballads, these poems are often complex in form and structure and present a story which is not so simple to interpret. A well-known example of a literary ballad is Coleridge's poem 'The Rime of the Ancient Mariner'.

The ballad 'Little Musgrave and the Lady Barnard' is known in several variant forms. In one version the tragic hero is called Matty Groves.

This ballad has been performed in various ways by contemporary folk singers and folk groups. Read through the ballad, then turn to **Responding** on page 43.

The Ballad of Little Musgrave _____

It fell upon a holy day
As many's in the year
Musgrave to the church did go
To see the fine ladies there.

5 And some were dressed in velvet red
And some in velvet pale
And then came in Lord Barnard's wife
The fairest of them all.

She cast an eye on the Little Musgrave
10 As bright as the summer's sun
Said Musgrave unto himself
'This lady's heart I've won.'

'I have loved you fair lady
for long and many's the day'.
15 'And I have loved you Little Musgrave
And never a word did say.'

'I've a bower in Bucklesford Bury
It's my heart's delight
I'll take you back there with me
20 If you lie in my arms tonight.'

But standing by was a little footpage
From the lady's coach he ran
'Although I am a lady's page
I am Lord Barnard's man.'

25 'My Lord Barnard will hear of this
Or whether I sink or swim.'
Everywhere the bridge was broke
He entered the water to swim.

'Oh my Lord Barnard, my Lord Barnard
30 You are a man of life
But Musgrave, he's at Bucklesford Bury
Asleep with your wedded wife.

'If this be true my little footpage,
This thing that you tell me
35 All the gold in Bucklesford Bury
I gladly will give to thee.'

'But if this be a lie, my little footpage,
This thing that you tell me
From the highest tree in Bucklesford Bury
40 A hanged you shall be.'

'Go saddle me the black,' he said,
'Go saddle me the grey.
And sound you not your horns,' he said,
'Lest our coming you betray.'

45 But there was a man in Lord Barnard's train
That loved the Little Musgrave
He blew his horn both loud and shrill
'Away Musgrave, away!'

'I think I hear the morning cock,
50 I think I hear the Jay
   I think I hear Lord Barnard's men
   I wish I was away.'

   'Lie still, lie still my Little Musgrave,
   Hug me from the cold
55 It's nothing but a shepherd lad
   A bringing his flock to fold.'

   'Is not your hawk upon its perch
   Your steed its oats and hay;
   And you a lady in your arms
60 And yet you go away?'

He's turned her around and he's kissed her twice
And then they fell asleep
When they awoke Lord Barnard's men
Were standing at their feet.

65 'How do you like my bed?' he said,
'And how do you like my sheets?
How do you like my fair lady
That lies in your arms asleep?'

'Its well I like your bed,' he said,
70 'And great it gives me pain,
I'd gladly give a hundred pound
To be on yonder plain.'

'Rise up, rise up, Little Musgrave
Rise up and then put on
75 It'll not be said in this country
I slayed a naked man.'

So slowly, so slowly he got up
So slowly he put on;
Slowly down the stairs
80 Thinking to be slain.

'There are two swords down by my side
And dear they cost my purse,
You can have the best of them
And I will take the worst.'

85 And the first stroke that Little Musgrave struck
It hurt Lord Barnard sore
But the next stroke Lord Barnard struck
Little Musgrave never struck more.

And then up spoke the lady fair
90 From the bed whereon she lay,
'Although you're dead, my Little Musgrave,
Still for you I'll pray.'

'How do you like his cheeks?' he said,
'How do you like his chin?
95 How do you like his dead body
Now there's no life within?'

'It's more I like his cheeks,' she cried,
'It's more I want his chin,
It's more I love that dead body
100 Than all your kith and kin.'

He's taken out his long, long sword
To strike the mortal blow,
Through and through the lady's heart
The cold steel it did go.

105 'A grave, a grave!' Lord Barnard cried,
'To put these lovers in;
But my lady had the upper hand
She came from better kin.'

'For I've just killed the finest knight
110 That ever rode a steed
And I've just killed the finest lady
That ever did a woman's deed.'

It fell upon a holy day,
As many's in the year,
115 Musgrave to the church did go
To see the fine ladies there.

Anonymous

Responding

When you have read the poem carefully, get into small groups of about
six people. Look carefully at the role of the narrator and think about the
delivery of the five characters' speeches.

In the same group organize a balloon debate in which the characters
have to defend their behaviour. The narrator can adopt the role of judge
and ensure that each character has the opportunity to speak.

Before presenting a case, each character will need to examine the poem
carefully in order to organize a defence. When all the characters have
been allowed to present a defence they can debate their actions and
behaviour with each other. The judge can decide where the greatest
fault lies, but must come to a decision based solely upon the quality of
debate offered by the different characters.

A5 Looking at Form and Structure

The sonnet

The sonnet is one of the most enduring forms in English poetry. The sonnet is essentially a fourteen-line poem. It developed in Italy in the fourteenth century but was used and developed by English poets from the early sixteenth century. There are several variations of the sonnet form, but the two main types are the Italian (or Petrarchan) sonnet and the English (or Shakespearean) sonnet.

The sonnet form has often been used for love poetry but many poets have used it to express other themes and ideas.

The Italian Sonnet has an **octave** (eight lines) and a **sestet** (six lines) with a rhyme scheme **abba abba cde cde**.

The English Sonnet is usually organized into three **quatrains** (four lines) with a concluding **couplet**. The rhyme scheme is based on the pattern **abab cdcd efef gg**. Sonnets are often written in sequences and present variations on a related theme. Shakespeare's **sonnet sequence** examines the themes of love and the ravages of time passing.

LX

Like as the waves make towards the pebbled shore,
So do our minutes hasten to their end;
Each changing place with that which goes before,
In sequent toil all forwards do contend.
5 Nativity, once in the main of light,
Crawls to maturity, wherewith being crowned,
Crookèd eclipses 'gainst his glory fight,
And time, that gave, doth now his gift confound.
Time doth transfix the flourish set on youth,
10 And delves the parallels in beauty's brow;
Feeds on the rarities of nature's truth,
And nothing stands but for his scythe to mow.
    And yet, to times in hope, my verse shall stand,
    Praising thy worth, despite his cruel hand.

William Shakespeare

Responding

◆ List all the things time does to us as we grow older, as suggested by this poem.

◆ In many of Shakespeare's sonnets the poet hopes that his art (his poetry) will triumph over time. What does he hope for in the couplet at the end of this sonnet?

◆ Shakespeare's sonnets are known either by their number or by their first line. When you have studied the poem carefully, suggest an appropriate title for it and then write a paragraph explaining the reason for your title.

Sonnets were very popular with the Romantic poets of the nineteenth century. Elizabeth Barrett Browning and Christina Rossetti both wrote sonnet sequences using the Italian sonnet as the basic form for their poetry.

How Do I Love Thee? _____

How do I love thee? Let me count the ways.
I love thee to the depth and breadth and height
My soul can reach, when feeling out of sight
For the ends of Being and Ideal Grace.
5 I love thee to the level of every day's
Most quiet need, by sun and candlelight.
I love thee freely, as men strive for Right;
I love thee purely, as they turn from Praise.
I love thee with the passion put to use
10 In my old griefs, and with my childhood's faith.
I love thee with a love I seemed to lose
With my lost saints, – I love thee with the breath,
Smiles, tears, of all my life! – and, if God choose,
I shall but love thee better after death.

Elizabeth Barrett Browning

Group work

When you have read the poem carefully and made notes, form a group with three or four other students and discuss issues raised by the poem. Think about:

◆ why the poem begins with a question
◆ why childhood is introduced into the poem
◆ the significance of lines 13–14
◆ the religious elements in the poem
◆ the use of the sonnet form to convey the emotions of the writer
◆ evidence that this was written by a female poet.

Record which questions have been satisfactorily answered, record points of agreement and disagreement, and make brief notes about the content of the discussion.

Now look at this sonnet by Christina Rossetti.

Sonnet _____

Remember me when I am gone away,
   Gone far away into the silent land;
   When you can no more hold me by the hand,
Nor I half turn to go yet turning stay.
5 Remember me when no more day by day
   You tell me of our future that you plann'd:
   Only remember me; you understand
It will be late to counsel then or pray.
Yet if you should forget me for a while
10   And afterwards remember, do not grieve:
   For if the darkness and corruption leave
   A vestige of the thoughts that once I had,
Better by far you should forget and smile
   Than that you should remember and be sad.

Christina Rossetti

Group work

Again, in a group with three or four other students, discuss points raised by your reading of this poem. Consider these questions in your discussions.

◆ Who is this poem addressed to?

◆ How would you describe the mood of the poem?

◆ Is there a contradiction between what the poet is asking in lines 1–8 and what she is asking in lines 9–14?

◆ What is the significance of lines 13–14?

In note form record the main issues covered in your group discussion and be ready to share these with other groups.

Now look at this modern poem in a variation of the sonnet form.

Transformation

Always I trip myself up when I try
To plan exactly what I'll say to you.
I should allow for how my feelings lie
Ready to leap up, showing what is true,

5 But in a way I never had designed.
How is it you are always ready when
Those linked ideas like beads within my mind,
Break from their thread and scatter tears again?

I am amazed, and distances depart,
10 Words touch me back to quiet. I am free
Who could not guess such misery would start

And stop so quickly, change the afternoon
And, far much more than that, transfigure me.
Trusting myself, I enter night, stars, moon.

Elizabeth Jennings

Group work

Use these points to help you in your discussion.

◆ Who is the poem addressed to?

◆ How effective are the images the poet uses to express the difficulties she has in communicating her feelings?

◆ What happens in lines 9–14? Why?

Comparisons

Look at 'How Do I Love Thee?', 'Sonnet' and 'Transformation'.

1 Make notes to describe what points these poems have in common and in what ways they are different. You might like to consider the following topics in your comparison.

◆ How similar are the sonnet forms used in these poems?

◆ Are there any similarities between the main themes of each sonnet?

◆ What are the similarities and differences in the poets' attitude to love and to their lovers?

◆ Which poem conveys the most emotion and how does it do this?

◆ In what ways are the content and tone of the twentieth-century sonnet very different from the nineteenth-century sonnets?

2 Use your notes above to help you write a comparison between the three sonnets.

3 Look again at the Shakespeare sonnet and the two nineteenth-century sonnets. All three sonnets are concerned with time and death in some way. Make notes comparing the sonnets using the following points to help you:

◆ the layout and appearance of each poem on the page

◆ the use of the sonnet form

◆ the subject matter in each poem

◆ the depth of emotion conveyed by each poem

◆ the message, if there is one, that the poet wishes to express

◆ the difference in attitude between Shakespeare and the two Victorian female poets, as revealed by these three poems.

A5 Looking at Form and Structure

Epitaphs

An epitaph is a piece of verse, or poem, that summarizes someone's life after his or her death. Originally an epitaph was meant as a funerary inscription. Epitaphs can be viewed as poetic forms in the sense that they all have similar subject matter. However, they do not follow a strict form in the way sonnets do. Many epitaphs are intended as serious reminders of a deceased person, but many others are humorous, or witty.

From Aberdeen

Here lies the bones of Elizabeth Charlotte
Born a virgin, died a harlot.
She was aye a virgin at seventeen
A remarkable thing in Aberdeen.

A Dentist

Stranger! Approach this spot with gravity!
John Brown is filling his last cavity.

MARIA J. TILDSLEY
1809 ~ 1841
Here lie I near the church
yard wall.
My life I hope you may recall.
Though of little consequence
to you
I did bring joy to quite
few

For Himself _____

Here lies Marc Conelly.
Who?

Marc Conelly

For His Wife _____

Here lies my wife
Here let her lie!
Now she's at rest
And so am I.

John Dryden

The following epitaph is inscribed on the tomb of George Routledge, who is buried beside the church at Lydford in Devon.

Epitaph in Lydford Churchyard _____

Here lies in a horizontal position the outside case of

GEORGE ROUTLEDGE, WATCHMAKER

Integrity was the mainspring and prudence
the regulator of all the actions of his life;
humane, generous and liberal,
His hand never stopped till he had relieved distress.

So nicely regulated were his movements that
he never went wrong, except when set going by
people who did not know his key.
Even then he was easily set right again.
He had the art of disposing his time so well,
till his hours glided away, his pulse
stopped beating.

He ran down November 14, 1801, aged 57
In hopes of being taken in hand by his Maker,
Thoroughly cleaned, repaired, wound up, and set
going in the world to come, when time shall be no more.

Writing

Write an imaginary epitaph for youself. Your epitaph does not have to be serious or morbid, you can make it witty and lighthearted if you wish. Try to include some biographical details in your verse and make your own personality and character shine through your writing.

A6 *Rhyme*

You have probably been surrounded by rhyming verses for as long as you can remember. Think of nursery rhymes or the lyrics of pop songs which you carry with you in your head. Do you think the rhymes help you to remember them?

Why rhyme?

When you're discussing rhyme in poetry it's important to think about *why* the poem rhymes and what effect the rhyme has. English poets have been writing poems that rhyme since the thirteenth century. Many nursery rhymes and songs that have been passed on by word of mouth through the generations use rhyme. Why do you think this is?

Here are some reasons why rhyme may be important.

◆ It gives a musical sound quality to verse.

◆ Rhymes may help us to remember verses and the stories or ideas in them.

◆ Rhymes give us a sense of security – we know or can guess what's coming next.

◆ Rhymes can shock us – if we're expecting a particular rhyme and we don't get it.

◆ Rhymes can make us laugh.

Look at the following three verses. Decide which of the three statements above are most applicable to each verse.

> Double, double toil and trouble
> Fire, burn; and, cauldron, bubble.

> *William Shakespeare*

Little Jack Horner
Sat in a corner
Eating his veal and ham pie
He pulled out a sliver
Of some mouse's liver
And most of the same mouse's eye

David Brazier

He who binds to himself a joy
Does the winged life destroy
But he who kisses the joy as it flies
Lives in eternity's sun rise.

William Blake

Look at the way the rhyme is identified in the poem below. This is the standard way of identifying a poem's rhyme scheme.

The Voice _____

Woman much missed, how you call to me, call to me,	**A**
Saying that now you are not as you were	**B**
When you had changed from the one who was all to me,	**A**
But as at first, when our day was fair.	**B**
Can it be you that I hear? Let me view you, then,	**C**
Standing as when I drew near to the town	**D**
Where you would wait for me: yes, as I knew you then,	**C**
Even to the original air-blue gown!	**D**
Or is it only the breeze, in its listlessness	**E**
Travelling across the wet mead to me here,	**F**
You being ever dissolved to wan wistlessness,	**E**
Heard no more again far or near?	**F**
Thus I: faltering forward,	**G**
Leaves around me falling,	**H**
Wind oozing thin through the thorn from norward,	**G**
And the woman calling.	**H**

Thomas Hardy

mead: meadow   **wan**: exhausted, pale   **wistlessness**: lacking energy
thorn: thorny shrubs or trees   **norward**: northerly direction

A7 *Rhythm*

Most poetry is written with a **rhythm** or a particular beat to it. The rhythm usually reinforces the content or subject matter. For instance, a poem which describes a lonely landscape in the evening may have a slow, stately rhythm:

> *When summer's end is nighing*
> *And skies at evening cloud . . .*

whereas a poem which captures the turmoil of battle will probably use a faster rhythm:

> *Storm'd at with shot and shell,*
> *Boldly they rode and well . . .*

When you read a poem for the first time, try to feel the beat. Exaggerate the emphasis of the beat in your mind and note if it is lively, jerky, sombre, stately, etc.

If you're discussing or writing about rhythm, remember to think about the way the rhythm mirrors the subject matter of the poem.

Activity 1

The poem 'Night Mail' by W. H. Auden was originally written to accompany a film produced by the Post Office. The fast beat used in this poem cleverly echoes the rhythm of an old-fashioned train.

Night Mail

(Commentary for a G.P.O. film)

This is the Night Mail crossing the Border,
Bringing the cheque and the postal order,

Letters for the rich, letters for the poor,
The shop at the corner, the girl next door.

5   Pulling up Beattock, a steady climb:
The gradient's against her, but she's on time.

Past cotton-grass and moorland boulder,
Shovelling white steam over her shoulder,

Snorting noisily, she passes
10 Silent miles of wind-bent grasses.

Birds turn their heads as she approaches,
Stare from bushes at her blank-faced coaches.

Sheep-dogs cannot turn her course;
They slumber on with paws across.

15 In the farm she passes no one wakes,
But a jug in a bedroom gently shakes.

W.H. Auden

Responding

1 Prepare a group reading of this poem which emphasizes the rhythm of the poem in a dramatic manner.

2 Write a short piece explaining how the rhythm of the poem matches its content.

Use examples from the poem.

Activity 2

Poetry which has been written primarily for live performance often relies upon beat or rhythm to stimulate a sense of vitality and directness.

Look at the following poem which uses a rap beat.

Baby-K Rap Rhyme

My name is Baby-K
An dis is my rhyme
Sit back folks
While I rap my mind;

5 Ah rocking with my homegirl,
My Mommy
Ah rocking with my homeboy,
My Daddy
My big sister, Les an
10 My Granny,
Hey dere people – my posse
I'm the business
The ruler of the nursery

poop po-doop
15 poop-poop po-doop
poop po-doop
poop-poop po-doop

Well, ah soaking up de rhythm
Ah drinking up my tea
20 Ah bouncing an ah rocking
On my Mommy knee
So happy man so happy

poop po-doop
poop-poop po-doop
25 poop po-doop
poop-poop po-doop

Wish my rhyme wasn't hard
Wish my rhyme wasn't rough
But sometimes, people
30 You got to be tough

Cause dey pumping up de chickens
Dey stumping down de trees
Dey messing up de ozones
Dey messing up de seas

35 Baby-K say, stop dis –
please, please, please

poop po-doop
poop-poop po-doop
poop po-doop
40 poop-poop po-doop

Now am splashing in de bath
With my rubber duck
Who don't like dis rhyme
Kiss my baby-foot
45 Babies everywhere
Join a Babyhood

Cause dey hotting up de globe, man
Dey hitting down de seals
Dey killing off de ellyies
50 For dere ivories
Baby-K say, stop dis –
please, please, please

poop po-doop
poop-poop po-doop
55 poop po-doop
poop-poop po-doop

Dis is my Baby-K rap
But it's a kinda plea
What kinda world
60 Dey going to leave fuh me?
What kinda world
Dey going to leave fuh me?
　　Poop po-doop.

Grace Nichols

Group work

1 When you have read the poem, organize yourself into a group
with at least three other people and prepare your own
performance of this poem. Recite the poem as a group,
emphasizing the rhythm, or perform it as rap with a musical
backing.

2 In groups, discuss whether or not you believe rap is a good
medium to use for a poem with a serious message like 'Baby-K
Rap Rhyme'.

3 Take one of the subjects below and in a group with two or three other students create your own rap poem.

- ◆ First Date
- ◆ Low Pay And No Work
- ◆ My Sport
- ◆ Our Town
- ◆ Tomorrow's World.

Remember to capture the rhythm of rap in your poem and be prepared to perform your work. If you can use a drum or musical backing this will be even better.

Identifying metre

The technical term for rhythm in poetry is **metre**. We work out the metre of a poem by working out which syllables in the line are stressed or unstressed. We mark stressed syllables ˋ and unstressed syllables ˘.

The most common metre in English poetry is **iambic** metre. The rhythm it employs has a beat like this:

$$te \, \textbf{Tum}, \, te \, \textbf{Tum}, \, te \, \textbf{Tum} \text{ etc.}$$

with the emphasis (stress) on the second syllable.

This line from Shakespeare's play *Macbeth* uses iambic metre:

> So foul and fair a day I have not seen.
> (te **Tum** te **Tum** te **Tum** te **Tum** te **Tum**)

and because there are 5 beats to the line it is called **iambic pentameter**.

John Milton's epic poem *Paradise Lost* also uses iambic pentameter as in these lines from Book IX when Adam speaks to Eve in the Garden of Eden:

> Not then mistrust, but tender love, enjoins
> That I should mind thee oft and mind thou me.

There are many different metres used in English poetry. Identifying and labelling these metres can be a rather technical matter. At this stage it is important that you are aware of a poem's rhythm and can describe it in your own way and explain why such a rhythm is being used.

It is fairly unusual for a poem to be written in the same metre all the way through. More often, a poet varies the rhythm in order to create a particular effect.

A8 Is it Poetry?

What are the main differences between prose and poetry? How easy is it to define what a poem actually *is*? Many poems are written in **free verse** (without definite verse patterns or rhyme schemes). Meanwhile, novels and other texts written in prose often use imagery, symbolism, personification and rhythm to create particular effects.

Activity

Look closely at the three extracts on the next page. One of these extracts is, in fact, a work of poetry laid out as prose. Only the shape and layout of the poem have been changed – everything else is exactly the same.

The other two passages are extracts from two different short stories and they are reproduced exactly as written in the short stories.

Writing

1 Read the three extracts carefully and then decide which extract you believe is really a poem written out as prose.

    When you have made your decision, rewrite the text in what you think might be its original poetic form. (The original poem was written in four-line verses, called **quatrains**.)

2 Write notes explaining why you selected the passage which you did, and then say what 'poetic techniques' you detected in the other texts.

3 Compare your rewritten text with those completed by other students in your class. Are you in agreement? Discuss your solutions.

4 What can you say about your rewritten text to explain why it is a poem? Think about line length, the shape of the poem on the page and the use of language.

A Though my mother was already two years dead Dad kept her slippers warming by the gas, put hot water bottles her side of the bed and still went to renew her transport pass. You couldn't just drop in. You had to phone. He'd put you off an hour to give him time to clear away her things and look alone as though his still raw love were such a crime. He couldn't risk my blight of disbelief though sure that very soon he'd hear her key scrape in the rusted lock and end his grief. He **knew** she'd just popped out to get the tea. I believe life ends with death, and that is all. You haven't both gone shopping; just the same, in my new black leather phone book there's your name and the disconnected number I still call.[1]

B   In the open, the smoke from the engine sank and cleaved to the rough grass. The fields were dreary and forsaken, and in the marshy strip that led to the whimsy, a reedy pit-pond, the fowls had already abandoned their run among the alders, to roost in the tarred fowl-house. The pit-bank looked up beyond the pond, flames like red sores licking its ashy sides, in the afternoon's stagnant light. Just beyond rose the tapering chimneys and the clumsy black headstocks of Brinsley Colliery. The two wheels were spinning fast up against the sky, and the winding engine rapped out its little spasms. The miners were being turned up.[2]

C Yes, the newspapers were right: snow was general all over Ireland. It was falling on every part of the dark central plain, on the treeless hills, falling softly upon the Bog of Allen and, farther westward, softly falling into the dark mutinous Shannon waves. It was falling, too, upon every part of the lonely churchyard on the hill where Michael Furey lay buried. It lay thickly drifted on the crooked crosses and headstones, on the spears of the little gate, on the barren thorns. His soul swooned slowly as he heard the snow falling faintly through the universe and faintly falling, like the descent of their last end, upon all the living and the dead.[3]

5 In small groups, look at page 156. Did you choose this extract?

[1] By Tony Harrison   [2] By D.H. Lawrence   [3] By James Joyce

A9 Comparing Poems

If you are studying poetry as part of an examination course you may be asked to compare two or more poems, either in examination conditions or as a piece of coursework.

Activity 1

Look at these poems by Phoebe Hesketh and James Berry.

Heatwave _____

Heat over all; not a lark can rise
Into the arching sun;
The moor like a lion sleeping lies –
Rough mane on burning stone.
5 Not a harebell shakes; the wild blue flags
Of wind are folded up.
Here on the hill the air is still
As water in a cup.   *Phoebe Hesketh*

Coming of the Sun _____

The sun came out in England today –
faces cracked wanting to smile.
Overcoats were guests overstayed.
Nakedness wanted to be the rage.

5 The sun came out echoing on:
people yearned for distant coastlines
and yearned for all good news;
neighbours stood at fences, asking.

The sun came out in England today.
10 Lambs leapt over each other on hillsides.   *James Berry*

Responding

1 Read each poem separately and make notes as you respond to it.

2 The poems you are asked to compare for your examination or coursework will probably have similar subject matter or similar themes. The poets may have different opinions or views about their subjects or they may approach the subject in different ways.

Make notes about the similarities and differences between these poems, using a copy of the chart opposite. Use the prompts to help you.

◆ Do the poems focus on the same subject matter? Are they about *exactly* the same thing?

◆ Where is each poem set?

◆ Have either of the poets placed themselves in the poem? (Note the reference in 'Heatwave' to 'here on the hill'.)

◆ What is each poet's attitude to the hot weather? How can you tell?

◆ Which poem do you prefer? Why?

◆ Look at the way the poets use images of nature or images of people. Why does each poet choose the images he/she does?

◆ Do the poems repeat any words or phrases? Why?

◆ How many verses has each poem? Do they rhyme? Why?

Writing

Using your notes, write a short comparison of these two poems.

Indicate any similarities between the subject matter and the techniques used by the poets. What differences are there between the poems?

	Similarities	Differences
Subject		
Setting		
Viewpoint		
Poet's attitude to the subject		
Your personal response		
Images		
(References to people)		
(References to nature)		
Form/Structure		
General points		

Activity 2

Look carefully at these poems by Edwin Brock and George MacBeth.

A Moment of Respect _____

Two things I remember about my grandfather:
his threadbare trousers, and the way he adjusted
his half-hunter watch two minutes every day.

When I asked why he needed to know the time so
5 exactly, he said a business man could lose a fortune
by being two minutes late for an appointment.

When he died he left two meerschaum pipes
and a golden sovereign on a chain. Somebody
threw the meerschaum pipes away, and
10 there was an argument about the sovereign.

On the day of his burial the church clock chimed
as he was lowered down into the clay, and all
the family advanced their watches by two minutes.

Edwin Brock

The Drawer

Their belongings were buried side by side
In a shallow bureau drawer. There was her
Crocodile handbag, letters, a brooch,
All that was in the bedside cupboard
5 And a small green jar she'd had for flowers.

My father's were in an envelope:
A khaki lanyard, crushed handkerchief,
Twelve cigarettes, a copying-pencil,
All he had on him when he was killed
10 Or all my mother wanted to keep.

I put them together, seven years ago.
Now that we've moved, my wife and I,
To a house of our own, I've taken them out.
Until we can find another spare drawer
15 They're packed in a cardboard box in the hall.

So this dead, middle-aged, middle-class man
Killed by a misfired shell, and his wife
Dead of cirrhosis, have left one son
Aged nine, aged nineteen, aged twenty-six,
20 Who has buried them both in a cardboard box.

George MacBeth

Responding

Make notes comparing the poems, using the points below to help you.
You may like to use a chart like the one on page 63.

◆ What is the subject matter of both poems?

◆ What is the viewpoint of each poet? (Have they placed themselves 'in the poems'?)

◆ In both poems the objects are vivid reminders of dead people. What is each poet's attitude to the objects? Why?

◆ What do the objects tell us about the people who owned them?

◆ Compare the last stanzas of each poem. What differences are there?

◆ What do the titles tell you about each poem?

Writing

Use your notes to help you to write a comparison of the two poems.

Activity 3

Look closely at this poem by the Irish poet, Patrick Kavanagh, then at the poem by Elizabeth Jennings on page 67.

In Memory Of My Mother _____

I do not think of you lying in the wet clay
Of a Monaghan graveyard; I see
You walking down a lane among the poplars
On your way to the station, or happily

5 Going to second Mass on a summer Sunday —
You meet me and you say:
'Don't forget to see about the cattle —'
Among your earliest words the angels stray.

And I think of you walking along a headland
10 Of green oats in June,
So full of repose, so rich with life —
And I see us meeting at the end of a town

On a fair day by accident, after
The bargains are all made and we can walk
15 Together through the shops and stalls and markets
Free in the oriental streets of thought.

O you are not lying in the wet clay,
For it is a harvest evening now and we
Are piling up the ricks against the moonlight
20 And you smile up at us — eternally.

Patrick Kavanagh

Responding

◆ Is there anything distinctly Irish in the content or vocabulary of this poem?

◆ Is the poem a lament for, or a celebration of, the poet's mother?

My Mother Dying Aged 87

You died as quietly as your spirit moved
All through my life. It was a shock to hear
Your shallow breathing and more hard to see
Your eyes closed fast. You did not wake for me
5 But even so I do not shed a tear.
Your spirit has flown free
Of that small shell of flesh. Grandchildren stood
Quietly by and it was they who gave
Most strength to us. They also loved you for
10 Your gentleness. You never made them fear
Anything. The memories you leave
Are happy times. You were

The one who gave me stamps and envelopes
And posted all my early poems. You had
15 Such faith in me. You could be firm and would
Curb tantrums, and would change an angry mood
With careful threats. I cannot feel too sad
Today for you were good

And that is what the kindly letters say.
20 Some are clumsy, some embarrass with
Lush piety but all will guide your ship
Upon a calm, bright ocean and we keep
Our eyes on it. It is too strong for death
And so we do not weep.

Elizabeth Jennings

Responding

◆ Why does Elizabeth Jennings 'not shed a tear' for her dead mother?
◆ How appropriate is the metaphor of the 'ship' in the last verse?

Discussion

◆ Which poem did you find the most moving or memorable?
◆ Were you surprised by any of the comments in them?
◆ Is the subject matter really the same in each poem?

◆ Is it significant that one appears to be written only a little time after the mother's death?

◆ Is it apparent that one poem is written by a man and the other by a woman?

Writing

Make notes comparing and contrasting the two poems. (Use the notes on page 147 to help you if you wish.)

Comparisons

1 Compare the poems in this unit with the poems in Activity 2 on pages 64–65. They are all about the death of a relative.

2 Extend your comparison to include a pre-twentieth century poem. This poem by Ben Jonson is about the death of his son. It was first published in 1616.

On My First Son _____

Farewell, thou child of my right hand, and joy;
My sin was too much hope of thee, loved boy.
Seven years thou wert lent to me, and I thee pay,
Exacted by thy fate, on the just day.
5 O, I could lose all father, now. For why
Will man lament the state he should envy?
To have so soon scap'd world's, and flesh's rage,
And if no other misery, yet age!
Rest in soft peace, and, asked, say here doth lie
10 Ben Jonson his best piece of poetry.
For whose sake, henceforth, all his vows be such,
As what he loves may never like too much.

Ben Jonson

Activity 4

The following poems by Wes Magee and Roger McGough both describe
people in a light-hearted and amusing way.

Big Aunt Flo

Every Sunday afternoon
She visits us for tea
And weighs-in somewhere between
A rhino and a flea.
5   (But closer to the rhino!)

Aunt Flo tucks into doughnuts,
Eats fruit cake by the tin.
Her stomach makes strange noises
Just like my rude friend, Flynn.
10   (Sounds more like a goat, really!)

Then after tea she heads for
The best chair in the room
And crashes on the cushions
With one resounding boom.
15   (You'd think a door had slammed!)

Flo sits on knitting needles
And snaps them with a crack.
She squashes dolls and jigsaws
Behind her massive back.
20   (And she doesn't feel a thing!)

But aunt Flo learned a lesson,
There's no doubt about that,
Last Sunday when she grabbed the chair
And sat down on our cat.
25   (Big Tom, a cat with a temper!)

The beast let out a wild yell
And dug his claws in . . . deep.
Poor Flo clutched her huge behind
And gave a mighty leap.
30   (She almost reached the ceiling!)

So now at Sunday teatime
Jam doughnuts going spare.
Dad winks, and asks where Flo is.
While Tom sleeps on *that* chair.
35   (And he's purring, the devil!)

Wes Magee

Responding

◆ Wes Magee creates a vivid picture of Aunt Flo – do you feel sorry for her at all? Why?

◆ Why does 'Dad wink' in the last verse?

W.P.C. Marjorie Cox

W.P.C. Marjorie Cox
brave as a lion
bright as an ox
is above all else, a girl.
5 Large of bosom
soft of curl.

Keeps in her dainty vanity case
diamante handcuffs, trimmed with lace,
a golden whistle, a silken hanky,
10 a photograph of a popstar manqué
(signed: 'To Marjorie, with love'),
a truncheon in a velvet glove.

W.P.C. Marjorie Cox
cute as a panda
15 in bobby sox.
Men queue to loiter with intent
for the pleasure of an hour spent
in her sweet custody.

Roger McGough

Responding

◆ How does McGough use the language in the poem to reinforce the fact that Marjorie Cox is a W.P.C.?

◆ Is there a serious message in this poem?

Comparisons

Explain what you find amusing in these two poems. Is the slapstick humour of 'Big Aunt Flo' more effective than the clever use of phrases and images in 'W.P.C. Marjorie Cox'?

Writing

◆ Imagine that Aunt Flo and Marjorie Cox read these poems. How would they react?

◆ Write the letters these two characters might send to the poets concerned to convey their feelings about the poems.

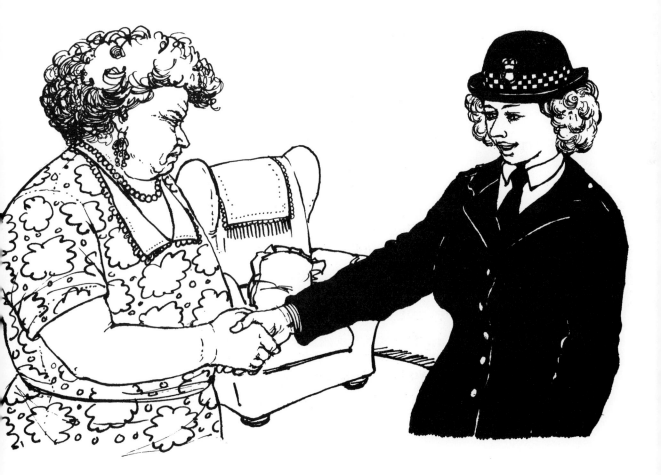

A9 Comparing Poems

Activity 5

The following poems by Dorothy Nimmo and Maya Angelou have very similar titles but how similar are the poems?

A Woman's Work _____

Will you forgive me that I did not run
to welcome you as you came in the door?
Forgive I did not sew your buttons on
and left a mess strewn on the kitchen floor?
5 A woman's work is never done
and there is more.

The things I did I should have left undone
the things I lost that I could not restore;
Will you forgive I wasn't any fun?
10 Will you forgive I couldn't give you more?
A woman's work is never done,
and there is more.

I never finished what I had begun,
I could not keep the promises I swore,
15 so we fought battles neither of us won
and I said, "Sorry!" and you banged the door.
A woman's work is never done
and there is more.

But in the empty space now you are gone
20 I find the time I didn't have before.
I lock the house and walk out to the sun
where the sea beats upon a wider shore
and woman's work is never done,
not any more.

Dorothy Nimmo

Responding

◆ Who do you think the poem is addressed to (who is the 'you' in the poem)?

◆ What is the poet saying about women's work in the first three verses? What has changed in the last verse?

Woman Work

I've got the children to tend
The clothes to mend
The floor to mop
The food to shop
5 Then the chicken to fry
The baby to dry
I got company to feed
The garden to weed
I've got the shirts to press
10 The tots to dress
The cane to be cut
I gotta clean up this hut
Then see about the sick
And the cotton to pick.

15 Shine on me, sunshine
Rain on me, rain
Fall softly, dewdrops
And cool my brow again.

Storm, blow me from here
20 With your fiercest wind
Let me float across the sky
'Til I can rest again.

Fall gently, snowflakes
Cover me with white
25 Cold icy kisses and
Let me rest tonight.

Sun, rain, curving sky
Mountain, oceans, leaf and stone
Star, shine, moon glow
30 You're all that I can call my own.

Maya Angelou

Responding

◆ Why do you think the first verse is longer than the others and has no punctuation?

◆ What is the poet asking for in the next four verses? Does the poem end on an optimistic note?

Comparisons

◆ What have the poems in common?

◆ After listing the chores women often have to do, both poems move on to suggest that life offers alternatives. What might these be?

◆ Which poem do you think is the most optimistic? Why?

◆ Can you find any evidence that Maya Angelou is an American poet?

Writing

◆ Write an essay comparing these two poems, explaining carefully their similarities and differences. Use the notes you made for **Comparisons** to help you.

◆ Write a poem which covers the same issues as these two poems but from a man's point of view.

Activity 6

Look closely at these poems by William Wordsworth and William Blake. Both poems deal with the development of London at the end of the eighteenth century.

Wordsworth's poem was written in 1800 and is clearly a poem in praise of a great city. London was a much smaller place in those days and the poem reveals that even from Westminster Bridge the countryside was not far away.

Composed upon Westminster Bridge _____

Earth has not anything to show more fair:
Dull would he be of soul who could pass by
A sight so touching in its majesty:
This City now doth, like a garment, wear
5 The beauty of the morning; silent, bare,
Ships, towers, domes, theatres, and temples lie
Open unto the fields, and to the sky;
All bright and glittering in the smokeless air.
Never did sun more beautifully steep
10 In his first splendour, valley, rock, or hill;
Ne'er saw I, never felt, a calm so deep!
The river glideth at his own sweet will:
Dear God! the very houses seem asleep;
And all that mighty heart is lying still!

William Wordsworth

Responding

What particular aspects of the city does Wordsworth find 'touching' in this poem?

Now read this poem by William Blake. The poem was published in 1794 and clearly expresses Blake's strong negative feelings about London.

London _____

I wander thro' each chartered street,
Near where the chartered Thames does flow,
And mark in every face I meet
Marks of weakness, marks of woe.

5 In every cry of every man,
In every infant's cry of fear,
In every voice, in every ban
The mind-forged manacles I hear.

How the chimney-sweeper's cry
10 Every blackening church appals;
And the hapless soldier's sigh
Runs in blood down palace walls.

But most thro' midnight streets I hear
How the youthful harlot's curse
15 Blasts the new-born infant's tear,
And blights with plagues the marriage hearse.

William Blake

chartered: a bill of rights, a royal document giving legal status to a city
ban: curse or swear word   **manacles**: handcuffs   **hapless**: unfortunate
harlot: prostitute

Comparisons

1 Compare Wordsworth's view of London with Blake's view of London. Think about:

   ◆ how each poet responds to the city
   ◆ the images each poet chooses to reflect his view of the city.

LONDON

I wander thro' each charter'd street,
Near where the charter'd Thames does flow
And mark in every face I meet
Marks of weakness, marks of woe,

In every cry of every Man,
In every Infants cry of fear,
In every voice; in every ban,
The mind-forg'd manacles I hear

How the Chimney-sweepers cry
Every blackning Church appalls,
And the hapless Soldiers sigh,
Runs in blood down Palace walls

But most thro' midnight streets I hear
How the youthful Harlots curse
Blasts the new born Infants tear
And blights with plagues the Marriage hearse

Imaginative response

These poems appear to contrast two views of London. They were written at almost the same time but the poets seem to be suggesting different messages.

1 Imagine Blake and Wordsworth were able to appear for a few minutes on a modern television chat show. In groups of three, produce a short role-play in which the host of the chat show encourages both poets to talk about their poems.

2 Look over the two poems again and then write two poems of your own. In one of them capture some aspect of a modern town or city that you find appealing. Consider locality, time of day and time of year when you construct your verse.

In your other poem reflect on some feature of present-day Britain that frustrates or saddens you. Perhaps you could focus on some part of contemporary Britain that you would like to change.

Compare 'Westminster Bridge' and 'London' with the following poem, which offers a more recent view of London.

Daily London Recipe _____

Take any number of them
you can think of,
pour into empty red bus
    until full,
5 and then push in
    ten more
Allow enough time
to get hot under the collar
before transferring into
10 multistorey building.
Leave for eight hours
and pour back into same bus
    already half full.
    Scrape remainder off.
15 When settled down
tip into terraced houses each
carefully lined with copy of
The Standard and Tit Bits.

Place mixture before open
20 television screen at 7 p.m.
and then allow to cool
in bed at 10.30 p.m.
May be served with
working overalls
25 or pinstripe suit.

Steve Turner

Activity 7

Look closely at 'The Fly', a poem written by the Czech poet Miroslav Holub and translated into English by George Theiner. The Battle of Crécy was fought between the English and French armies in 1346.

The Fly

She sat on a willow-trunk
watching
part of the battle of Crécy,
the shouts,
5 the gasps,
the groans,
the tramping and the tumbling.

During the fourteenth charge
of the French cavalry
10 she mated
with a brown-eyed male fly
from Vadincourt.

She rubbed her legs together
as she sat on a disembowelled horse
15 meditating
on the immortality of flies.

With relief she alighted
on the blue tongue
of the Duke of Clervaux.

20 When silence settled
and only the whisper of decay
softly circled the bodies

and only
a few arms and legs
25 still twitched jerkily under the trees,

she began to lay her eggs
on the single eye
of Johann Uhr,
the Royal Armourer.

30 And thus it was
that she was eaten by a swift
fleeing
from the fires of Estrées.

Miroslav Holub

Responding

◆ Is the fly the real subject of this poem?
◆ What message is conveyed by lines 30–33 of this poem?
◆ Can you see a structure to this poem?

Now look closely at the following poem by Keith Douglas.
Vergissmeinnicht is the German word for forget-me-not. Douglas was a
soldier in the Second World War and he fought with the British army in
the deserts of North Africa. Afterwards he was posted to Europe where
he was killed on 9th June 1944.

Vergissmeinnicht _____

Three weeks gone and the combatants gone
returning over the nightmare ground
we found the place again, and found
the soldier sprawling in the sun.

5 The frowning barrel of his gun
overshadowing. As we came on
that day, he hit my tank with one
like the entry of a demon.

Look. Here in the gunpit spoil
10 the dishonoured picture of his girl
who has put: *Steffi. Vergissmeinnicht*
in a copybook gothic script.

We see him almost with content
abased, and seeming to have paid
15 and mocked at by his own equipment
that's hard and good when he's decayed.

But she would weep to see today
how on his skin the swart flies move;
the dust upon the paper eye
20 and the burst stomach like a cave.

For here the lover and killer are mingled
who had one body and one heart.
And death who had the soldier singled
has done the lover mortal hurt.

Keith Douglas

Responding

◆ Who is the 'she' referred to in line 17?

◆ Why is the dead German called 'the soldier' in line 23, and then 'the lover' in line 24?

◆ What is the signifiance of the title of this poem?

◆ What is so ironic about Douglas writing this poem in memory of the dead soldier?

Comparisons

Use your notes to write a response to the following question:

How are our attitudes to war shaped by each of these poems?

Use these prompts to help you.

◆ Consider the way in which both poems are organized and structured.

◆ Reflect on the reference to the fly in each poem.

◆ Examine the role of the poet's voice and viewpoint and the message about war which each poem conveys.

◆ Do you find one poem to be more effective than the other and, if so, why?

A10 *Poetry in Context*

In your English examination or for English coursework you may be asked questions which focus on the culture or tradition in which the poet is writing. An example of this kind of question might be as follows:

> *Choose two poems and explain how the poets have used words and specific details to:*
> * *make the people interesting*
> * *capture aspects of their particular culture*
> * *give the poems distinctive atmosphere.*

or

> *Choose two poems and explain how the poets use local customs and traditions to emphasize powerful emotions.*

When you're faced with questions like this the important thing to remember is *not* simply to repeat facts you have learned about the poem's or poet's background. You're not being asked to *know* about the poet's culture but to explore what the poem tells you.

Activity 1

Read this poem by Nissim Ezekiel. It is set in India.

Night of the Scorpion _____

I remember the night my mother
was stung by a scorpion. Ten hours
of steady rain had driven him
to crawl beneath a sack of rice.
5 Parting with his poison – flash
of diabolic tail in the dark room –
he risked the rain again.

The peasants came like swarms of flies
and buzzed the name of God a hundred times
10 to paralyse the Evil One.
With candles and with lanterns
throwing giant scorpion shadows
on the mud-baked walls
they searched for him: he was not found.
15 They clicked their tongues.
With every movement that the scorpion made
his poison moved in Mother's blood, they said.
May he sit still, they said.
May your suffering decrease
20 the misfortune of your next birth, they said.
May the sum of evil
balanced in this unreal world
against the sum of good
become diminished by your pain.
25 May the poison purify your flesh
of desire, and your spirit of ambition,
they said, and they sat around
on the floor with my mother in the centre,
the peace of understanding on each face.
30 More candles, more lanterns, more neighbours,
more insects, and the endless rain.
My mother twisted through and through,
groaning on a mat.
My father, sceptic, rationalist,
35 trying every curse and blessing,
powder, mixture, herb and hybrid.
He even poured a little paraffin
upon the bitten toe and put a match to it.
I watched the flame feeding on my mother.
40 I watched the holy man perform his rites
to tame the poison with an incantation.
After twenty hours
it lost its sting.

My mother only said
45 Thank God the scorpion picked on me
and spared my children.

Nissim Ezekiel

Responding

1 What aspects of 'Night of the Scorpion' tell you that it is written in India?

2 What does the poem tell you about:

◆ the peasants

◆ the mother

◆ the father?

3 Explain how the details in the poem help you to visualize the scene.

4 Imagine a similar incident happening in this country. (For example, someone is bitten by an adder when out walking.) What would happen here?

Activity 2

Now read this poem by Felix Mnthali.

My Uncle E. P. M. Harawa _____

Don't call it perfect timing
when my uncle emerges
from nowhere
leading a procession
5   of men, women and children
bearing groundnuts, potatoes
and fresh maize

With shoulders upright
and marching as to war
10 he has always been
the source of wonders among men –
always emerging from nowhere
to stand where we needed him
at the moment that we needed him –

15 What would Malawians
around the miming towns
of Selukwe, Shabani, Guinea Fowl
have done without him?

I see him now
20 in his white coat
stethoscope slung on his shoulders
muttering 'Oh yes'
through rows of patients
in the hospital at Camper Down

25 I see him again
Sundays this time
right in front of the congregation
and to this day up there in
Mbulunji, a tower of strength
30 to the Church of Central Africa, Presbyterian.

Will our children ever follow
the love that sends a man
at the break of day
to gather the choicest maize and the choicest fruit
35 and wait close to the roadside
to emerge quietly
as the van to Zomba
comes in view?

Don't call it perfect timing:
40 he has always been
where he was to be
at the minute he was to be
like his ancestor Kajimerere
who it is said
45 explained his origins by saying,
'I grew out of this land.'

Felix Mnthali

Responding

1 What sort of person was Uncle E. P. M. Harawa? How does the poet
feel about him?

2 Explain how the poet creates pictures to help you build an
impression of Harawa.

3 Why does the poet repeat the phrase 'Don't call it perfect timing' in
line 39? What does he mean by it?

4 What does the poem tell you about the poet's cultural background? Think about:

◆ how the people live and where they work

◆ what they eat

◆ places where they gather together.

Does the poem help you to build a picture of the people Harawa helped?

How important do you think tradition is to this poem?

Comparisons

1 Which poem do you prefer and why?

2 Which poem helps you build the clearest picture of the culture in which it is set?

Why?

Writing

Now return to the questions at the beginning of this unit on page 82 and answer one question as an extended piece of writing.

B1 *William Wordsworth*

William Wordsworth was born in Cockermouth, Cumbria in 1770. His father was a lawyer but both his parents were dead by 1783. In 1791 Wordsworth went to France where he greatly admired the political ideals which had brought about the French Revolution. He later became very disillusioned by the bloodshed caused by this event.

He moved to Somerset in 1795 with his sister Dorothy and they lived close to the poet Coleridge. Wordsworth and Coleridge worked closely together and in 1798 produced a book of poems called *Lyrical Ballads.*

In 1799 William and Dorothy Wordsworth moved back to live in the Lake District. William Wordsworth married Mary Hutchinson in 1802. They had five children, two of whom died in infancy. Wordsworth was made Poet Laureate in 1843 and he died in 1850.

Even in his own lifetime, Wordsworth's reputation as a poet was much debated. His early poetry was a rejection of the conventional literary styles which had gone before. Many of these poems were criticized and rejected by other writers at the time because they dealt with everyday subjects and were written in deliberately simple language. He believed that the human spirit could grow by experiencing the beauty of nature and reflecting on these experiences. He tried to write in a style which reflected the simplicity and naturalness of everyday speech.

My Heart Leaps Up

My heart leaps up when I behold
   A rainbow in the sky:
So was it when my life began;
So is it now I am a man;
5 So be it when I shall grow old,
   Or let me die!
The Child is father of the Man;
And I could wish my days to be
Bound each to each by natural piety.

William Wordsworth

Responding

◆ What is so special about the rainbow in this poem?
◆ What does Wordsworth mean by 'The Child is father of the Man' (line 7)?

Sonnet

Milton! thou shouldst be living at this hour:
England hath need of thee: she is a fen
Of stagnant waters: altar, sword, and pen,
Fireside, the heroic wealth of hall and bower,
5 Have forfeited their ancient English dower
Of inward happiness. We are selfish men;
Oh! raise us up, return to us again;
And give us manners, virtue, freedom, power.
Thy soul was like a Star, and dwelt apart;
10 Thou hadst a voice whose sound was like the sea:
Pure as the naked heavens, majestic, free,
So didst thou travel on life's common way,
In cheerful godliness; and yet thy heart
The lowliest duties on herself did lay.

William Wordsworth

Responding

◆ Milton was a famous English poet. He was also a Puritan, who wrote many papers on church matters and political issues. He died in 1674. Why does Wordsworth refer to him in this poem?

◆ Can you imagine what might upset Wordsworth if he were living in England today?

Daffodils

I wandered lonely as a cloud
That floats on high o'er vales and hills,
When all at once I saw a crowd,
A host, of golden daffodils:
5   Beside the lake, beneath the trees,
Fluttering and dancing in the breeze.

Continuous as the stars that shine
And twinkle on the milky way,
They stretched in never-ending line
10 Along the margin of a bay:
Ten thousand saw I at a glance,
Tossing their heads in sprightly dance.

The waves beside them danced; but they
Out-did the sparkling waves in glee:
15 A poet could not but be gay,
In such a jocund company:
I gazed – and gazed – but little thought
What wealth the show to me had brought:

For oft, when on my couch I lie
20 In vacant or in pensive mood,
They flash upon that inward eye
Which is the bliss of solitude;
And then my heart with pleasure fills,
And dances with the daffodils.

William Wordsworth

Responding

◆ What phrases capture Wordsworth's delight at seeing the daffodils?

◆ What effect does the memory of the daffodils have upon Wordsworth?

William Wordsworth

To the Cuckoo

O blithe New-comer! I have heard,
I hear thee and rejoice.
O Cuckoo! shall I call thee Bird,
Or but a wandering Voice;

5 While I am lying on the grass
Thy twofold shout I hear;
From hill to hill it seems to pass
At once far off, and near.

Though babbling only to the Vale,
10 Of sunshine and of flowers,
Thou bringest unto me a tale
Of visionary hours.

Thrice welcome, darling of the Spring!
Even yet thou art to me
15 No bird, but an invisible thing,
A voice, a mystery;

The same whom in my schoolboy days
I listened to; that Cry
Which made me look a thousand ways
20 In bush, and tree, and sky.

To seek thee did I often rove
Through woods and on the green;
And thou wert still a hope, a love;
Still longed for, never seen.

25 And I can listen to thee yet;
Can lie upon the plain
And listen, till I do beget
That golden time again.

O blessed Bird! the earth we pace
30 Again appears to be
An insubstantial, faery place;
That is fit home for Thee!

William Wordsworth

Responding

◆ Why does the sound of the cuckoo mean so much to Wordsworth?

◆ What do 'To the Cuckoo' and 'Daffodils' have in common?

She Dwelt _____

She dwelt among the untrodden ways
    Beside the springs of Dove,
A Maid whom there were none to praise
    And very few to love:

5 A violet by a mossy stone
    Half hidden from the eye!
– Fair as a star, when only one
    Is shining in the sky.

She lived unknown, and few could know
10   When Lucy ceased to be:
But she is in her grave, and, oh,
    The difference to me!

William Wordsworth

Responding

◆ This is one of five love poems known as the 'Lucy poems'. The real identity of Lucy has never been clarified. In what sense was she like a 'violet'?

◆ What effect is created by lines 11–12 of the poem?

The Prelude

The Prelude is a very long autobiographical poem. Wordsworth uses the poem to revisit his childhood and to trace his development as a poet. 'Residence in London' is an extract from *The Prelude*.

Residence in London _____

– And first the look and aspect of the place
The broad high-way appearance, as it strikes
on Strangers of all ages, the quick dance
Of colours, lights and forms, the Babel din
5 The endless stream of men, and moving things,
From hour to hour the illimitable walk
Still among streets with clouds and sky above,
The wealth, the bustle and the eagerness,
The glittering Chariots with their pamper'd Steeds,
10 Stalls, Barrows, Porters; midway in the Street
The Scavenger, who begs with hat in hand,
The labouring Hackney Coaches, the rash speed,
Of coaches travelling far, whirl'd on with horn
Loud blowing, and the sturdy Drayman's Team,
15 Ascending from some Alley of the Thames
And striking right across the crowded Strand
Till the fore horse veer round with punctual skill:
Here there and everywhere a weary throng
The Comers and the Goers face to face,
20 Face after face; the string of dazzling Wares,
Shop after shop, with Symbols, Blazon'd Names,
And all the Tradesman's honours overhead . . .

William Wordsworth

Responding

◆ How informative is this description of London as it was in Wordsworth's time?

◆ What do you notice about the punctuation of this extract? What effect does this create?

Overview

◆ How simple and natural is the language used by Wordsworth in his poetry? Find examples to illustrate your answer.

◆ This selection of Wordsworth's poetry is quite varied. How easy is it to see links between the poems? What are they?

◆ Most of these poems were written in the first half of the nineteenth century. List the evidence which shows that these poems were written over 150 years ago.

Writing

◆ Do you believe the emotions expressed in Wordsworth's poems are overstated or do they add to the power of the poetry? Think about the serious tone of the poems compared with the subjects they deal with.

◆ From this selection of Wordsworth's poetry, would you describe him as a 'Nature Poet'? Think about
   – the number of topics which describe and deal with nature
   – other topics covered in these poems.

Imaginative response

◆ Imagine you could make a film of Wordsworth's life and poetry. Write a description of the film you want to make, including details of location and soundtrack.

B2 *Christina Rossetti*

Christina Rossetti was born in England in 1830. Her father had moved from Italy in 1824. Throughout the Victorian period the Rossetti family were very much involved in new artistic movements. Christina was active in publishing prose writings and poetry and her brother Dante Gabriel Rossetti was a well-known painter and poet.

Christina Rossetti never married but was engaged for a time to the painter James Collinson. The engagement was broken off in 1850 because Collinson rejoined the Roman Catholic Church. Christina Rossetti was a devout member of the Anglican Church. For most of her life she suffered from ill-health and her condition became severe before her death in 1894.

Christina Rossetti's *Poetical Works* were published ten years after her death, by her brother, W. M. Rossetti. Rossetti's poetry includes verses written for children, religious poetry and love poetry. Her work focuses on the theme of frustrated love and is often subdued and sombre in tone.

Up-Hill

Does the road wind up-hill all the way?
    Yes, to the very end.
Will the day's journey take the whole long day?
    From morn to night, my friend.

5 But is there for the night a resting-place?
    A roof for when the slow, dark hours begin.
May not the darkness hide it from my face?
    You cannot miss that inn.

Shall I meet other wayfarers at night?
10   Those who have gone before.
Then must I knock, or call when just in sight?
    They will not keep you standing at that door.

Shall I find comfort, travel-sore and weak?
    Of labour you shall find the sum.
15 Will there be beds for me and all who seek?
    Yea, beds for all who come.

Christina Rossetti

Responding

◆ In this poem, life is compared to a journey – what does the poem suggest about this journey?

◆ Because Christina Rossetti was a religious person, what other type of journey might be suggested by this poem?

◆ How effective is the simple alternate question-and-answer structure of the poem?

A Birthday

My heart is like a singing bird
    Whose nest is in a watered shoot;
My heart is like an apple-tree
    Whose boughs are bent with thickset fruit;
5 My heart is like a rainbow shell
    That paddles in a halcyon sea;
My heart is gladder than all these
    Because my love is come to me.

Raise me a dais of silk and down;
10   Hang it with vair and purple dyes;
Carve it in doves and pomegranates,
    And peacocks with a hundred eyes;
Work it in gold and silver grapes,
    In leaves and silver fleurs-de-lys;
15 Because the birthday of my life
    Is come, my love is come to me.

Christina Rossetti

Responding

◆ What is being celebrated in this poem?

◆ Explain the various ways in which repetition is used in this poem. How effective is it?

◆ What is the effect of the similes used in the first verse?

A Dirge

Why were you born when the snow was falling?
You should have come to the cuckoo's calling,
Or when grapes are green in the cluster,
Or at least when lithe swallows muster
5   For their far off flying
    From summer dying.

Why did you die when the lambs were cropping?
You should have died at the apples' dropping,
When the grasshopper comes to trouble,
10 And the wheat-fields are sodden stubble,
    And all winds go sighing
    For sweet things dying.

Christina Rossetti

Responding

◆ A dirge is a song of mourning – what is so significant about the death lamented here?

◆ Can you explain why the poem is so neatly organized into two verses?

The Bourne

Underneath the growing grass,
    Underneath the living flowers,
    Deeper than the sound of showers;
    There we shall not count the hours
5 By the shadows as they pass.

Youth and health will be but vain,
    Beauty reckoned of no worth:
    There a very little girth
    Can hold round what once the earth
10 Seemed too narrow to contain.

Christina Rossetti

Responding

◆ Can you guess what a 'bourne' is from reading the poem?

◆ Why does the poet say 'we shall not count the hours . . .' in line 4?

In the bleak mid-winter,
Frosty wind made moan,
Earth stood hard as iron,
Water like a stone;
5 Snow had fallen, snow on snow,
Snow on snow,
In the bleak mid-winter
Long ago.

Our God, Heaven cannot hold Him
10 Nor earth sustain;
Heaven and earth shall flee away
When he comes to reign:
In the bleak mid-winter
A stable-place sufficed
15 The Lord God Almighty
Jesus Christ.

Enough for Him, whom cherubim
Worship night and day,
A breastful of milk
20 And a mangerful of hay;
Enough for Him, whom angels
Fall down before,
The ox and ass and camel
Which adore.

25 Angels and archangels
May have gathered there,
Cherubim and seraphim
Thronged the air.
But only His mother
30 In her maiden bliss
Worshipped the Beloved
With a kiss.

What can I give Him,
Poor as I am?
35 If I were a shepherd
I would bring a lamb;
If I were a Wise Man
I would do my part, –
Yet what I can I give him, –
40 Give my heart.   *Christina Rossetti*

Christina Rossetti

Responding

◆ This is a very popular Christmas carol – what phrases in the poem remind us of the poverty of the stable in which Christ was born?

◆ Can you explain the statement that is being made in the last verse?

Overview

◆ If you assume that this selection of poems is typical of Christina Rossetti's work, what can you deduce about her life and interests?

◆ Is there anything in this selection of poetry that signals that the poems were written by a female poet?

◆ How much of the subject matter of this poetry still has relevance today?

Writing

◆ Can you detect in this selection of poetry the fact that Christina Rossetti lived a sheltered, artistic life? Think about:
   – the subjects she deals with
   – the serious tone of her poems.

◆ Would you know from reading these poems that Christina Rossetti lived in the nineteenth century? Think about:
   – her viewpoint in the poems
   – the language and vocabulary used.

Imaginative response

◆ Using the poems as a basis, write a magazine article in which you present a picture of the sort of person you think Christina Rossetti was. Think about:
   – the issues covered in her poetry
   – the autobiographical details revealed in the poems.

B3 *Wilfred Owen*

Wilfred Owen was born in 1893 at Oswestry, Shropshire, where his father was a station-master. He was educated at Shrewsbury Technical College before going to London University. In 1913 he went to Bordeaux to teach English and returned to England in 1915 to join the army. He was a junior officer at the Battle of the Somme where he suffered trench fever and concussion. He was sent to a military hospital in Edinburgh where he met the poet Siegfried Sassoon. Sassoon encouraged Owen to continue writing his poetry about the war and in 1918 Owen was sent back to France to join his regiment. Wilfred Owen was awarded the Military Cross for bravery in 1918 and he was killed on November 4th, one week before the armistice.

Most of Owen's poems were written in a short space of time in 1917 and 1918. Only five of his poems were published in his lifetime.

Almost all of Wilfred Owen's surviving poetry describes life as a soldier in the trenches. His poems are written with grim realism.

The Send Off

Down the close darkening lanes they sang their way
To the siding-shed,
and lined the train with faces grimly gay.

Their breasts were stuck all white with wreath and spray
5 As men's are, dead.

Dull porters watched them, and a casual tramp
Stood staring hard,
Sorry to miss them from the upland camp.

Then, unmoved, signals nodded, and a lamp
10 Winked to the guard.

So secretly, like wrongs hushed-up, they went.
They were not ours:
We never heard to which front these were sent;

Nor there if they yet mock what women meant
15 Who gave them flowers.

Shall they return to beatings of great bells
In wild train-loads?
A few, a few, too few for drums and yells,
May creep back, silent, to village wells,
20 Up half-known roads.

Wilfred Owen

Responding

◆ Can you explain why the soldiers' return is likely to be so different from their departure?

◆ What is the significance of the flowers given to the soldiers?

The Sentry

We'd found an old Boche dug-out, and he knew,
And gave us hell; for shell on frantic shell
Lit full on top, but never quite burst through.
Rain, guttering down in waterfalls of slime,
5 Kept slush waist-high and rising hour by hour,
And choked the steps too thick with clay to climb.
What murk of air remained stank old, and sour
With fumes from whizz-bangs, and the smell of men
Who'd lived there years, and left their curse in the den,
10 If not their corpses . . .

     There we herded from the blast
Of whizz-bangs, but one found our door at last, –
Buffeting eyes and breath, snuffing the candles.
And thud! flump! thud! down the steep steps came thumping
15 And splashing in the flood, deluging muck,
The sentry's body; then, his rifle, handles
Of old Boche bombs, and mud in ruck on ruck.
We dredged it up, for dead, until he whined
'O sir, my eyes, – I'm blind – I'm blind, – I'm blind!'
20 Coaxing, I held a flame against his lids
And said if he could see the least blurred light
He was not blind; in time he'd get all right.
'I can't', he sobbed. Eyeballs, huge-bulged like squids',
Watch my dreams still, – yet I forgot him there
25 In posting Next for duty, and sending a scout
To beg a stretcher somewhere, and flound'ring about
To other posts under the shrieking air.

Those other wretches, how they bled and spewed,
And one who would have drowned himself for good, –
30 I try not to remember these things now.
Let Dread hark back for one word only: how
Half listening to that sentry's moans and jumps,
And the wild chattering of his broken teeth,
Renewed most horribly whenever crumps
35 Pummelled the roof and slogged the air beneath, –
Through the dense din, I say, we heard him shout
'I see your lights!' But ours had long died out.

Wilfred Owen

Responding

◆ What reasons can you give to explain why Wilfred Owen says he 'forgot' about the wounded sentry?

◆ What elements of this poem do you find most shocking?

Disabled

He sat in a wheeled chair, waiting for dark,
And shivered in his ghastly suit of grey,
Legless, sewn short at elbow. Through the park
Voices of boys rang saddening like a hymn,
5 Voices of play and pleasure after day,
Till gathering sleep had mothered them from him.

About this time Town used to swing so gay
When glow-lamps budded in the light blue trees,
And girls glanced lovelier as the air grew dim, –
10 In the old times, before he threw away his knees.
Now he will never feel again how slim
Girls' waists are, or how warm their subtle hands.
All of them touch him like some queer disease.

There was an artist silly for his face,
15 For it was younger than his youth, last year.
Now, he is old; his back will never brace;
He's lost his colour very far from here,
Poured it down shell-holes till the veins ran dry,
And half his lifetime lapsed in the hot race
20 And leap of purple spurted from his thigh.

One time he liked a blood-smear down his leg,
After the matches, carried shoulder-high.
It was after football, when he'd drunk a peg,
He thought he'd better join. – He wonders why.
25 Someone had said he'd look a god in kilts,
That's why; and may be, too, to please his Meg;
Aye, that was it, to please the giddy jilts
He asked to join. He didn't have to beg;
Smiling they wrote his lie: aged nineteen years.
30 Germans he scarcely thought of; all their guilt,
And Austria's, did not move him. And no fears
Of Fear came yet. He thought of jewelled hilts
For daggers in plaid socks; of smart salutes;
And care of arms; and leave; and pay arrears;
35 *Esprit de corps;* and hints for young recruits.
And soon he was drafted out with drums and cheers.

Wilfred Owen

Some cheered him home, but not as crowds cheer Goal.
Only a solemn man who brought him fruits
Thanked him; and then enquired about his soul.

40 Now, he will spend a few sick years in Institutes,
And do what things the rules consider wise,
And take whatever pity they may dole.
To-night he noticed how the women's eyes
Passed from him to the strong men that were whole.
45 How cold and late it is! Why don't they come
And put him into bed? Why don't they come?

Wilfred Owen

Responding

◆ What reasons are suggested for this soldier's eagerness to go to war?

◆ Can you list all the things this young man has lost because of the war?

◆ Are there any signs of anger in this poem? What is the 'lie' referred to in line 29?

Anthem for Doomed Youth _____

What passing-bells for these who die as cattle?
– Only the monstrous anger of the guns.
    Only the stuttering rifles' rapid rattle
Can patter out their hasty orisons.
5 No mockeries now for them; no prayers nor bells,
    Nor any voice of mourning save the choirs, –
The shrill, demented choirs of wailing shells;
    And bugles calling for them from sad shires.
What candles may be held to speed them all?
10   Not in the hands of boys but in their eyes
Shall shine the holy glimmers of goodbyes.
    The pallor of girls' brows shall be their pall;
Their flowers the tenderness of patient minds,
And each slow dusk a drawing-down of blinds.

Wilfred Owen

Responding

◆ What references can you find in the poem to the Christian Church?

◆ Can you explain line 14 of the poem?

Overview

◆ Considering Wilfred Owen was an officer in the Army, are you surprised by his poems? Why?

◆ How might other soldiers have reacted to Owen's poems?

◆ Would you describe Owen's poetry as direct and powerful? Why?

◆ What is the role of women or girls in these poems?

Writing

◆ Write an essay outlining the different aspects of war touched upon in this selection of poetry by Wilfred Owen.

Think about:
– the fear and anxiety of men leaving home and going to war
– the grim brutality of warfare
– the casualties of war
– the effect war has on the way human beings think and feel.

◆ Although he was a soldier, would you say that Owen is an anti-war poet? Write an argument to support your views.

Think about:
– whether Owen makes war seem exciting
– whether there are any positive comments about war in these poems
– the language used to describe scenes and events
– the message conveyed by each poem.

Imaginative response

Imagine you are a fellow-soldier who served with Wilfred Owen. Write an account of the sort of person he was and the events that prompted his poetry.

B4   *Ted Hughes*

Ted Hughes was born in Yorkshire in 1930. He was educated at Cambridge University where he met the American writer, Sylvia Plath. They were married in 1956 and they influenced each other's work until Sylvia Plath's suicide in 1963. Ted Hughes' first volume of poetry *The Hawk in the Rain* was published in 1957. In 1984 he was made Poet Laureate and he is now living and writing in North Devon.

As a young boy, Ted Hughes spent much time fishing and hunting and his poetry reflects his interest in animals and the world of nature. But Ted Hughes' poetry is not sentimental about the countryside; his descriptions are harsh and uncompromising. Similarly the language used in his poetry is direct and forceful. Over the last ten or twelve years Hughes has increasingly been involved in environmental issues and the subject matter of much of his poetry remains centred on the landscape in which he lives.

Ted Hughes

Pike

Pike, three inches long, perfect
Pike in all parts, green tigering the gold.
Killers from the egg: the malevolent aged grin.
They dance on the surface among the flies.

5 Or move, stunned by their own grandeur
Over a bed of emerald, silhouette
Of submarine delicacy and horror.
A hundred feet long in their world.

In ponds, under the heat-struck lily pads –
10 Gloom of their stillness:
Logged on last year's black leaves, watching upwards.
Or hung in an amber cavern of weeds

The jaws' hooked clamp and fangs
Not to be changed at this date;
15 A life subdued to its instrument;
The gills kneading quietly, and the pectorals.

Three we kept behind glass,
Jungled in weed: three inches, four,
And four and a half: fed fry to them –
20 Suddenly there were two. Finally one

With a sag belly and the grin it was born with.
And indeed they spare nobody.
Two, six pounds each, over two feet long,
High and dry and dead in the willow-herb -

25 One jammed past its gills down the other's gullet:
The outside eye stared: as a vice locks –
The same iron in this eye
Though its film shrank in death.

A pond I fished, fifty yards across,
30 Whose lilies and muscular tench
Had outlasted every visible stone
Of the monastery that planted them –

Stilled legendary depth:
It was as deep as England. It held
35 Pike too immense to stir, so immense and old
That past nightfall I dared not cast

But silently cast and fished
With the hair frozen on my head
For what might move, for what eye might move.
40 The still splashes on the dark pond,

Owls hushing the floating woods
Frail on my ears against the dream
Darkness beneath night's darkness had freed,
That rose slowly towards me, watching.

Ted Hughes

Responding

◆ What characteristics of the pike make it an efficient killer
according to this poem?

◆ Can you explain the sense of menace and fear created in lines
41–44?

Ted Hughes

Harvest Moon

The flame-red moon, the harvest moon,
Rolls along the hills, gently bouncing,
A vast balloon,
Till it takes off, and sinks upward
5 To lie in the bottom of the sky, like a gold doubloon.

The harvest moon has come,
Booming softly through heaven, like a bassoon.
And earth replies all night, like a deep drum.

So people can't sleep,
10 So they go out where elms and oak trees keep
A kneeling vigil, in a religious hush.
The harvest moon has come!

And all the moonlit cows and all the sheep
Stare up at her petrified, while she swells
15 Filling heaven, as if red hot, and sailing
Closer and closer like the end of the world

Till the gold fields of stiff wheat
Cry 'We are ripe, reap us!' and the rivers
Sweat from the melting hills.

Ted Hughes

Responding

◆ What characteristics of the moon do you find most striking in this poem?

◆ Why is the comparison of the moon with a 'gold doubloon' so effective?

Ted Hughes

February 17th

A lamb could not get born. Ice wind
Out of a downpour dishclout sunrise. The mother
Lay on the mudded slope. Harried, she got up
And the blackish lump bobbed at her back-end
5 Under her tail. After some hard galloping,
Some manoeuvring, much flapping of the backward
Lump head of the lamb looking out,
I caught her with a rope. Laid her, head uphill
And examined the lamb. A blood-ball swollen
10 Tight in its black felt, its mouth gap
Squashed crooked, tongue stuck out, black-purple,
Strangled by its mother. I felt inside,
Past the noose of mother-flesh, into the slippery
Muscled tunnel, fingering for a hoof,
15 Right back to the port-hole of the pelvis.
But there was no hoof. He had stuck his head out too
    early
And his feet could not follow. He should have
Felt his way, tip-toe, his toes
20 Tucked up under his nose
For a safe landing. So I kneeled wrestling
With her groans. No hand could squeeze past
The lamb's neck into her interior
To hook a knee. I roped that baby head
25 And hauled till she cried out and tried
To get up and I saw it was useless. I went
Two miles for the injection and a razor.
Sliced the lamb's throat-strings, levered with a knife
Between the vertebrae and brought the head off
30 To stare at its mother, its pipes sitting in the mud
With all earth for a body. Then pushed
The neck-stump right back in, and as I pushed
She pushed. She pushed crying and I pushed gasping.

And the strength
35 Of the birth push and the push of my thumb
Against that wobbly vertebra were deadlock,
A to-fro futility. Till I forced
A hand past and got a knee. Then like
Pulling myself to the ceiling with one finger
40 Hooked in a loop, timing my effort
To her birth push groans, I pulled against
The corpse that would not come. Till it came.
And after it the long, sudden, yolk-yellow
Parcel of life
45 In a smoking slither of oils and soups and syrups –
And the body lay born, beside the hacked-off head.

Ted Hughes

Responding

◆ What aspects of this poem do you find most shocking?
◆ How significantly does this poem depart from the traditional view of lambing?

Hill-Stone was Content

To be cut, to be carted
And fixed in its new place.

It let itself be conscripted
Into mills. And it stayed in position
5 Defending this slavery against all.

It forgot its wild roots
Its earth-song
In cement and the drum-song of looms.

And inside the mills mankind
10 With bodies that came and went
Stayed in position, fixed like the stones
Trembling in the song of the looms.

And they too became four-cornered, stony

In their long, darkening stand
15 Against the guerrilla patience
Of the soft hill-water.

Ted Hughes

Responding

- How do the people who work in the mills resemble the stones used in constructing the mills?
- Why is there a reference to 'soft hill-water' in line 16?

Overview

- To what extent do you think this selection of poetry could only have been written by a male poet?
- Do you think the view of the world presented in these poems is unnecessarily hard and unyielding? Why?
- Do any aspects of these poems shock or surprise you? Why?
- What evidence is there that Hughes is a man who has chosen to live close to the earth?

Writing

- To what extent does the poetry of Ted Hughes present you with a different way of seeing the world? Think about:
  - the way animals are described in the poems
  - the unusual topics which are described
  - the fact that even everyday objects can be viewed differently.
- What is special about the vocabulary and language used in Ted Hughes' poetry? Think about:
  - the harshness of the words used
  - the uncompromising way in which he describes events
  - the colour and vividness of the imagery used in the poems.

Imaginative response

Imagine you are going to write an article on Ted Hughes. Write a letter to him in which you question him about his life and poetry.

B5 *Seamus Heaney*

Seamus Heaney is arguably the finest poet writing in English at the moment. He is an Irishman and was born in Co. Derry in Northern Ireland in 1939. He was educated at the Queen's University of Belfast and was a teacher there for several years before moving to live in Co. Wicklow in the Republic of Ireland. Between 1989 and 1994 Seamus Heaney was the Professor of Poetry at Oxford University and in 1995 he was awarded the Nobel Prize for Literature.

Heaney's early work reflects his rural childhood but with the publication of *North* in 1975 he began to address the violence in Northern Ireland and to link the sectarian killings with prehistoric murder victims found in Danish peat bogs. His more recent work touches upon his relationship with his family and friends and draws upon stories from Irish legends.

Honeymoon Flight _____

Below, the patchwork earth, dark hems of hedge,
The long grey tapes of road that bind and loose
Villages and fields in casual marriage:
We bank above the small lough and farmhouse

5 And the sure green world goes topsy-turvy
As we climb out of our familiar landscape.
The engine noises change. You look at me.
The coastline slips away beneath the wing-tip.

And launched right off the earth by force of fire,
10 We hang, miraculous above the water,
Dependent on the invisible air
To keep us airborne and to bring us further.

Ahead of us the sky's a geyser now.
A calm voice talks of cloud yet we feel lost.
15 Air-pockets jolt our fears and down we go.
Travellers, at this point, can only trust.

Seamus Heaney

Responding

◆ How significant is line 16 of this poem?

◆ In what ways are the couple leaving 'a familiar landscape'?

A Constable Calls

His bicycle stood at the window-sill,
The rubber cowl of a mud-splasher
Skirting the front mudguard,
Its fat black handlegrips

5   Heating in sunlight, the 'spud'
Of the dynamo gleaming and cocked back,
The pedal treads hanging relieved
Of the boot of the law.

His cap was upside down
10 On the floor, next his chair.
The line of its pressure ran like a bevel
In his slightly sweating hair.

He had unstrapped
The heavy ledger, and my father
15 Was making tillage returns
In acres, roods, and perches.

Arithmetic and fear.
I sat staring at the polished holster
With its buttoned flap, the braid cord
20 Looped into the revolver butt.

'Any other root crops?
Mangolds? Marrowstems? Anything like that?'
'No.' But was there not a line
Of turnips where the seed ran out

25 In the potato field? I assumed
Small guilts and sat
Imagining the black hole in the barracks.
He stood up, shifted the baton-case

Further round on his belt,
30 Closed the domesday book,
Fitted his cap back with two hands,
And looked at me as he said goodbye.

A shadow bobbed in the window.
He was snapping the carrier spring
35 Over the ledger. His boot pushed off
And the bicycle ticked, ticked, ticked.

Seamus Heaney

Responding

◆ In what lines or phrases can you detect a sense of fear or anxiety?

◆ What hints are there that Heaney is recollecting an event from childhood?

The Grauballe Man

As if he had been poured
in tar, he lies
on a pillow of turf
and seems to weep

5 the black river of himself.
The grain of his wrists
is like bog oak,
the ball of his heel

like a basalt egg.
10 His instep has shrunk
cold as a swan's foot
or a wet swamp root.

His hips are the ridge
and purse of a mussel,
15 his spine an eel arrested
under a glisten of mud.

The head lifts,
the chin is a visor
raised above the vent
20 of his slashed throat

that has tanned and toughened.
The cured wound
opens inwards to a dark
elderberry place.

25 Who will say 'corpse'
to his vivid cast?
Who will say 'body'
to his opaque repose?

And his rusted hair,
30 a mat unlikely
as a foetus's.
I first saw his twisted face

in a photograph
a head and shoulder
35 out of the peat,
bruised like a forceps baby,

but now he lies
perfected in my memory,
down to the red horn
40 of his nails,

hung in the scales
with beauty and atrocity:
with the Dying Gaul
too strictly compassed

45 on his shield,
with the actual weight
of each hooded victim,
slashed and dumped.   *Seamus Heaney*

Responding

◆ Is there any reason to think that the photograph Heaney saw of the
Grauballe man is the same as the one shown opposite?

◆ Can you suggest what connection there might be between the subject
of this poem and the recent events in Northern Ireland?

Seamus Heaney

The sonnet below comes from a sequence of eight sonnets in which Seamus Heaney records the death of his mother.

Sonnet No. 3

When all the others were away at Mass
I was all hers as we peeled potatoes.
They broke the silence, let fall one by one
Like a solder weeping off the soldering iron:
5 Cold comforts set between us, things to share
Gleaming in a bucket of clean water.
And again let fall. Little pleasant splashes
From each other's work would bring us to our senses.

So while the parish priest at her bedside
10 Went hammer and tongs at the prayers for the dying
And some were responding and some crying
I remembered her head bent towards my head,
Her breath in mine, our fluent dipping knives –
Never closer the whole rest of our lives.

Seamus Heaney

Responding

◆ Why does the poet recall a childhood memory in this poem?

◆ How would you describe the poet's attitude to the Catholic church in this poem?

Overview

◆ To what extent are people important in this selection of Heaney's poetry?

◆ Would you support the view that much of Heaney's poetry originates from simple, everyday events? Why?

◆ How clear is it that Seamus Heaney is a contemporary Irish poet?

Seamus Heaney

Writing

◆ How well does Heaney convey a sense of place in his poetry? Think about:
- the way he refers to sounds, smells and visual images in his poetry
- the personal details he describes when responding to a scene or an incident.

◆ How far does Seamus Heaney's subject matter and language reveal that the history and culture of the people of Northern Ireland are very important to him? Think about:
- the detail with which he describes everyday scenes
- the subjects he chooses to write about
- the references to religion and killing.

Imaginative response

Imagine you have to introduce Seamus Heaney at a poetry reading. Write a short speech to introduce him and his work.

B6 *Liz Lochhead*

Liz Lochhead was born in 1947 in Motherwell, Scotland. After finishing at school she went to art college in Glasgow and then worked for a while as an art teacher. In 1978 she was awarded a Writers' Exchange Fellowship and gave up teaching to concentrate on her writing. Since producing *Memo for Spring* in 1972, Liz Lochhead has produced several books of poetry.

Liz Lochhead also writes plays, raps and songs and she very much enjoys performing her own work. She has written poetry in a variety of styles – some of her work captures her own Scottish dialect. Liz Lochhead's poetry reflects the culture and society in which she lives and she is clearly a poet who sees the world from a woman's point of view. Much of her poetry is witty and there is often a sharp edge to her work.

Man on a Bench

This old man
has grown year-weary
no joy in changing seasons, just
another sodden summer
5 another corny old autumn
and another winter
to leave him cold.

Liz Lochhead

Responding

◆ Does 'Man on a Bench' contain any hint of sympathy for the man?

◆ What effect is created by the adjectives which describe the seasons?

Revelation

I remember once being shown the black bull
when a child at the farm for eggs and milk.
They called him Bob – as though perhaps
you could reduce a monster
5 with the charm of a friendly name.
At the threshold of his outhouse, someone
held my hand and let me peer inside.
At first, only black
and the hot reek of him. Then he was immense,
10 his edges merging with the darkness, just
a big bulk and a roar to be really scared of,
a trampling and a clanking tense with the chain's jerk.
His eyes swivelled in the great wedge of his tossed head.
He roared his rage. His nostrils gaped.

15 And in the yard outside,
oblivious hens picked their way about.
The faint and rather festive tinkling
behind the mellow stone and hasp was all they knew
of that Black Mass, straining at his chains.
20 I had always half-known he existed –
this antidote and Anti-Christ his anarchy
threatening the eggs, well rounded, self-contained –
and the placidity of milk.

I ran, my pigtails thumping on my back in fear,
25 past the big boys in the farm lane
who pulled the wings from butterflies and
blew up frogs with straws.
Past throned hedge and harried nest,
scared of the eggs shattering –
30 only my small and shaking hand on the jug's rim
in case the milk should spill.

Liz Lochhead

Responding

◆ In what sense is the event described in the poem a 'revelation'?
◆ Why does Liz Lochhead mention the hens in the yard and the boys
in the farm lane in this poem?

Of course
everybody's mother always and
so on . . .

Always never
5 loved you enough
or too smothering much.

Of course you were the Only One, your
mother
a machine
10 that shat out siblings, listen

everybody's mother
was the original Frigid-
aire Icequeen clunking out
the hardstuff in nuggets, mirror-
15 slivers and ice-splinters that'd stick
in your heart.

Absolutely everyone's mother
was artistic when she was young.

Everyone's mother
20 was a perfumed presence with pearls, remote
white shoulders when she
bent over in her ball dress
to kiss you in your crib.

Everybody's mother slept with the butcher
25 for sausages to stuff you with.

Everyone's mother
mythologised herself. You got mixed up
between dragon's teeth and blackmarket stockings.

Naturally
30 she failed to give you
Positive feelings
about your own sorry
sprouting body (it was a bloody shame)

but she did
35 sit up all night sewing sequins
on your carnival costume

so you would have a good time

and she spat
on the corner of her hanky and scraped
40 at your mouth with sour lace till you squirmed

so you would look smart

And where
was your father all this time?
Away
45 at the war, or
in his office, or any-
way conspicuous for his
Absence, so

what if your mother did
50 float around above you
big as a barrage balloon
blocking out the light?

Nobody's mother can't not never do nothing right.

Liz Lochhead

Responding

◆ How would you describe the tone of this poem?
◆ Which images:
   – reflect what mothers tend to say about themselves?
   – reflect 'everybody's' impression of a perfect mother?
   – suggest mothers might be inadequate?
◆ If this is a poem about motherhood, what does Liz Lochhead have to
   say about fathers?
◆ Why is line 53 so important in expressing what the poet really thinks
   about mothers?

What-I'm-Not Song

I'm not your Little Woman
I'm not your Better Half
I'm not your nudge, your snigger
Or your belly laugh.

5 I'm not Jezebel
And I'm not Delilah
I'm not Mary Magdalen
Or the Virgin Mary either.

Not a Novice or a Nun
10 Nor a Hooker or a Stripper
Not Super Shirley Conran
Not Jill the Ripper.

No I'm no Scissor-Lady –
I won't snip at your . . . locks.
15 I'm not a siren, you're not obliged
To get off my rocks.

Not Medusa, not Medea
And, though my tongue may be salty
I'm not the Delphic sybil –
20 Or Sybil Fawlty

I'm not Poison Ivy
You can throw away the lotion
I'm not your Living Doll
I'm not Poetry In Motion.

25 And if selling Booze and Cars
Involves my body being used, well . . .
I'm not Queen Victoria
But I'm not amused.

And if you don't like my body
30 You can sodding well lump it –
I'm not a Tart-with-a-Golden-Heart
Or Thinking Man's Crumpet.

I'm not your Woman of Achievement
Not your Slimmer of the Year
35 I'm not Princess Diana . . .
No Frog Princes 'ere!

I'm not little Ms Midler
I'm not little Miss Muffet
Make me An Offer I Can't Refuse –
40 And I'll tell you to stuff it!

'Cos I'm not your Little Woman
I'm not your Lady Wife
I'm not your Old Bag
Or the Love of Your Life –

45 No, I'm not your Little Woman
Not your Better Half
I'm not your Nudge, your Snigger
Or your Belly Laugh!

Liz Lochhead.

Responding

◆ What important message about women is being conveyed in 'What-I'm-Not Song'?

◆ What everyday phrases used to describe women do you recognize in this poem? Can you make a list of others not used here?

Men says My Boss
are definitely more dependable
and though even in these days of equal pay
men tend to come a wee bitty more expensive
5 due to the added responsibility a man tends to have
in his jobspecification
Well for instance you can depend on a man not to get
pregnant.
My Boss says men are more objective.
10 Catch a man bitching
about healthhazards and conditions
and going out on strike over no papertowels in the toilet
or nagging over the lack of day nursery facilities
My Boss says as far as he's concerned a crèche is a
15   motor accident in Kelvinside
and any self respecting woman should have a good man
to take care of her so it's only pinmoney anyway
and that's bound to come out in the attitude.
Well a man isn't subject to moods
20 or premenstrual tension a guy
isn't going to phone in sick with some crap about
    cramps.
My Boss says a man rings in
with an upset stomach and you know either
25 he means a hangover or else his brother
managed to get him a ticket for Wembley.

You know where you are with a man.

Liz Lochhead

Responding

◆ To what extent have you come across some of the views expressed in
this poem? How far do you agree with them?

◆ What makes the Boss say 'You know where you are with a man'?

◆ Imagine an interview this Boss may have with a prospective female
employee.

Overview

◆ To what extent would you describe Liz Lochhead as a humorous poet? To what extent do you think her poems have a dark side? Why?

◆ What do you find striking or distinctive about the way Liz Lochhead uses language in her poetry?

◆ Would you want to disagree with any of the points conveyed in the poems? Why?

Writing

◆ What have you enjoyed most when reading Liz Lochhead's poetry? Think about:
  – humour
  – how the poems relate to you
  – how Liz Lochhead uses language in her poetry.

◆ How female-centred is Liz Lochhead's writing? Think about:
  – the topics she deals with
  – how she expresses her views
  – her manner in expressing her views
  – the way she views men and the language of men
  – how she uses language.

Imaginative response

Liz Lochhead has given a live poetry performance in a working men's club. Make a transcript of the question-and-answer session which might follow.

B7 *Grace Nichols*

Grace Nichols was born in the Caribbean, in Georgetown, Guyana in 1950. She worked in the Caribbean as a journalist and reporter until she moved to Britain in 1977. She now lives and writes in Sussex. Her first book of poetry was published in 1983, the year she won the Commonwealth Poetry Prize.

As well as being a poet who enjoys performing her own poetry, Grace Nichols also writes novels and compiles poetry anthologies for younger readers. Her poetry celebrates life with a particular warmth. Grace Nichols' Caribbean origins are clearly in evidence in the language and phrasing of many of her poems. She is now one of Britain's best-known female poets.

Beauty

Beauty
is a fat black woman
walking the fields
pressing a breezed
5 hibiscus
to her cheek
while the sun lights up
her feet

Beauty
10 is a fat black woman
riding the waves
drifting in happy oblivion
while the sea turns back
to hug her shape.

Grace Nichols

Responding

◆ Why has Grace Nichols used the word 'fat' in a poem celebrating beauty?

◆ Can you explain why the Beauty described here is more than just a visual beauty?

Holding My Beads _____

Unforgiving as the course of justice
Inerasable as my scars and fate
I am here
a woman . . . with all my lives
5 strung out like beads
                          before me

It isn't privilege or pity
that I seek
It isn't reverence or safety
quick happiness or purity
                          but

10 the power to be what I am/   a woman
charting my own futures/   a woman
holding my beads in my hand

Grace Nichols

Responding

◆ What is it Grace Nichols says she is seeking in this poem?

◆ Why are beads referred to in the title and again in the last line?

139

Me good friend Beverley
Come to England. She was three.
She born in Jamaica, but seh,
Dis ya she country.
5 She ancestor blood help fe build it,
Dat is history.
Dih black presence go back
Two, three century.

She seh she fadder
10 Was minding he own business
Back in Jam-country,
Wid he lickle piece-o-land
An he lickle donkey
When dey sen he fe enlist
15 In de British Army.
Yes, he hads was to fight
Fe dis ya country.
Dey even give he medal fe bravery.

So policeman na come
20 Wid no brutality.
Mister Repatriation, yuh know,
You will haffi kill she
Cause she na go no whey
Dis ya she country,
25 Summer is hearts
An she dread de wintry
But she have she lickle flat
And she have she lickle key.

She seh she like it fine
30 She a pop wid style
You can never put she back inna no woodpile
Or she bun it to de ground

She seh she went to Uncle Sam
For a six-week vacation,
35 But after three weeks
She homesick fe England.

When de plane mek a touch-down
She feel so happy,
She feel she a come home,
40 Dis ya she country.
If dey think repatriation
Dem will haffi kill she.

De odder day
Wan ole English lady stop she,
45 Seh, 'Miss are you on holiday?'
Bev seh, 'Me not on holiday,
Me a live right hey.
Me na plan fe go no whey.'

De ole lady open she eye, surprisedly,
50 Bev seh, 'Is Black British dey call we.'
She seh, 'I don't mean to be unkind
But leh me tell you lickle history –
You see all dis big fat architectry?
In it is de blood of my ancestry.
55 Dih black presence go back
Two, three century.
Don't look at me so bemusedly.'

Bev seh, 'In any case, you been my country first,
So we come back inna kinda reverse.
60 Isn't life funny? Dis ya. Dis ya history.
O mek we tek a lickle walk,
It so nice an sunny.
Summer is hearts,
An a dread de wintry.
65 But a have me lickle flat
An a have me lickle key.
You want to come in
For a lickle cup-o-tea?'

Grace Nichols

Responding

◆ Is this a poem simply about a woman called Beverley? What else does it address?

◆ Why did the 'English lady' ask Bev if she was 'on holiday'?

Praise Song for My Mother _____

You were
water to me
deep and bold and fathoming

You were
5   moon's eye to me
pull and grained and mantling

You were
sunrise to me
rise and warm and streaming

10 You were
the fishes red gill to me
the flame tree's spread to me
the crab's leg/the fried plantain smell
                        replenishing replenishing
15 Go to your wide futures, you said

Grace Nichols

Responding

◆ What does 'Praise Song for My Mother' celebrate about the poet's mother?

◆ Are there any surprising comparisons in this poem?

On Her Way to Recovery _____

My thirteen-year-old daughter
is now taller than me.
Illness seemed to have stretched her a bit.

She, who was on her back
5 for four days and four nights,
feverish, heavy limbed, uneating,

Got up this morning
pulled on her sneakers, my long red dressing gown,
and went out into the garden.

10 'Don't worry,' she says,
coming suddenly into the room
where I'm lying, 'I dressed warm.'

Startled. Pleased.
I glance up at the red-robed gazelle
15 on her way to recovery.

Grace Nichols

Responding

◆ How well does this poem link with the previous poem?

◆ What effect is gained by calling her daughter a 'red-robed gazelle' in line 14?

Overview

◆ How significant is the mother-figure in this selection of Grace Nichols' poetry?

◆ Is it obvious that Grace Nichols enjoys performing her poetry? Why?

◆ Would you argue that the lack of male characters in these poems narrows their scope and interest? Why?

Writing

◆ By reference to Grace Nichols' poems can you show that she has a simple and direct approach to the subject of her poetry? Think about:
  - the clear simple message gained from each poem
  - the way she explores the subject matter with uncomplicated language
  - her use of everyday speech.

◆ What have you enjoyed most in this selection of poetry by Grace Nichols? Think about:
  - humour
  - how the poems relate to you
  - the clear message gained from each poem
  - how she uses language.

Imaginative response

Imagine you have to present the poetry of Grace Nichols to another class. Prepare a booklet with extracts of her poetry and write a commentary to go with the pieces you have chosen. Illustrate your booklet if you like.

C   *Writing about Poetry*

This section gives you advice on how to plan and write your essays. There are suggestions to help with preparing a coursework assignment, ideas for coursework and advice about writing on poetry in timed conditions.

Writing about a single poem

When you approach a new poem, remember the following points.

1   Don't panic – everything you want to write about is there in the poem itself. Read it a few times and look at it closely.

2   Ask some initial questions about the poem.

 ◆ Where is it set?

 ◆ What is happening?

 ◆ Who is talking?

 ◆ What do you feel about the poem on a first reading?

3   Read the poem carefully line by line and stanza by stanza. Annotate your copy of the poem. Ask yourself questions about it as you read and think about the following points.

 ◆ **Tone:** What is the mood of the poem?

 ◆ **Language:** What do you notice about vocabulary and punctuation? Does the poem use imagery? How effective are its images? How do the images relate to what the poet is saying?

 ◆ **The way the poem is organized:** What do you notice about layout? Is the poem divided into verses? Does it rhyme? Are the lines long or short or both? How does the shape of the poem match its content?

 ◆ **Your response:** What do you like or dislike about the poem so far?

Don't feel you need mention something about all of these points for every poem you write about! The points are there to help trigger your own thoughts. The most important thing is to relax, read the poem closely, enjoy it and write about what you find in the poem.

Planning your writing

The easiest way to write about a single poem is to follow the order of the poem itself. However, you must make sure you do not start writing too soon and just think of things to say as you go. You need to have an overview of your thoughts about the poem before you begin writing.

Plan 1

Introduction
Remember to respond to the question. Give an overview of your response to the poem and indicate your main thoughts.

First paragraph
If the *form* of the poem is important you may want to discuss it here before talking about each verse in detail.

Middle paragraphs
Write about each verse in turn. Look carefully at language and imagery and say how the language reflects the content. Include your own personal response to the poem too.

Final paragraph
Go back to the question and summarize the main points of your response.

A more demanding way to organize your essay is to plan it around key ideas.

Plan 2

Introduction
Remember to address the question. Give an overview of your response to the poem and indicate your main thoughts.

Paragraph two
Look at the poem's form and structure and how they relate to the content.

Paragraph three
Look at the language and imagery and how they relate to the content.

Paragraph four
Bring out any other important points which occur to you.

Ending
Summarize your main points and your personal response to the poem.

Writing a comparison

The easiest way to write about two poems is to deal with one poem first then the other. You will still need to have planned your thoughts about similarities and differences in advance because you will need to refer backwards and forwards between the two poems. (See page 63.)

Plan 1

Introduction

Introduce the main points of comparison. Refer to the subject matter of each poem and state the main similarities and differences. Discuss your personal response to the poems if you wish.

First section

Write about the first poem. As you write follow the order of the poem from the title to the last line. As you go discuss the subject of the poem and the poet's attitude to the subject, referring to details of language and imagery. Then discuss the layout or form. Don't forget about the other poem! Talk about similarities and differences where they occur.

Second section

Write about the second poem in the same way you did with the first. Refer back to the first poem, discussing similarities and differences.

Final section

Summarize the points of comparison and contrast. State which poem most appealed to you and which poem you thought was most effective.

A more demanding way is to structure your essay around main points of comparison and contrast as shown in the plan overleaf. This method will help you to focus on similarities and differences all the way through your essay.

Plan 2

Introduction
Introduce the main similarities or differences between the poems.

Paragraph 2
Describe the subject matter of each poem and the poet's attitudes to the subject.

Paragraph 3
Talk about each poet's use of language and imagery. Remember to say *why* each poet has chosen the images he/she has.

Paragraph 4
Compare each poet's use of structure and form. What is the layout of each poem? Do the poems have a regular form?

Paragraph 5
Discuss any other similarities and differences.

Paragraph 6
Say which poem you prefer and which you think is the most effective.

Whichever way you decide to structure your essay it is vital that you support your views by referring closely to the text and by using carefully chosen quotations.

Poetry in coursework

If you are studying English or English Literature as an examination course then it is quite likely that you will be expected to submit a poetry assignment for part of your coursework requirements. Some Examination Boards make this a compulsory element of the coursework.

The precise nature of the poetry assignment will normally be decided by your teacher and will depend upon which poetry texts you have studied. Although it is impossible to predict the exact task you will be given for coursework there are several ways your assignment may be organized:

1 You may be asked to consider and compare a selection of poems written by one poet.

2 You may be asked to compare the work of two or more poets to see what they have in common.

3 You may be asked to see how different poets respond to one theme, or subject – for instance war, love, nature, childhood, school and so on.

If you have been studying longer poems you may be expected to write a comparison between two long poems.

Preparing and writing your assignment

It is impossible to tell you how to prepare your own particular assignment but there are some general points that you may find helpful.

◆ When you know the details of the assignment you have been given, read the poems carefully. Make sure you give yourself plenty of time to study the poems before writing the assignments.

◆ Become familiar with the poems by making notes around them (see pages 8, 36, 157). If possible, try to discuss the poetry with other people – this often helps to clarify points.

◆ When you are happy that you know the poetry well enough, consider the question or topic that you have been asked to write about. **Think** about the question by brain-storming your ideas, or use a spider diagram to stimulate your response to the topic.

◆ After you have begun to generate some ideas about the assignment, you need to organize and plan your written response. Try to make your plan logical and clear. Note which poems you will be using and assemble quotations to support your views.

◆ Keep your plan simple. You may make notes for your assignment, rather like a shopping list.

◆ Write a rough draft of your assignment. Try to keep to your plan, but don't stop to check spellings or find exact quotes. Just write it! While it is going well, keep writing.

◆ When you have finished the rough draft, look over it and consider it carefully. **Edit it.** Have you left out anything important? Have you repeated yourself? Have you made your points clearly enough? Did you end your writing with a definite conclusion?
Be prepared to change anything that isn't quite right.

◆ Check over the spelling, punctuation and grammar of your work. Go back to the poetry and make sure the references to particular poems and the quotations are correct.

◆ Now write your final draft. This draft will be read by your teacher and an examiner, so check it carefully. Make sure the work is presented neatly and clearly.

Look over your final draft once more before submitting it as part of your coursework.

Suggested assignments

1   Look at the poetry of Ted Hughes in this book and compare it with the poetry of William Wordsworth.
    Do they deal with similar subjects? Do they treat these subjects in the same way? Explain whose poetry you prefer and why.

2   Compare the work of Christina Rossetti with that of Grace Nichols and Liz Lochhead. Is there a clear difference between the nineteenth-century poetry of Rossetti and the modern poetry of Nichols and Lochhead? Look at the subject matter written about and the way each poet deals with it.

3   Wilfred Owen once wrote 'My subject is war and the pity of war'. To what extent does his poetry reveal the horror and misery of war?

4   From the poems you have studied, what has impressed you about the way different poets have dealt with the environment?

5   Compile an anthology of extracts of your favourite poems. Select your extracts carefully, describe the poems they come from and then explain why you like them.

6   Look first at the poems written in the twentieth century and then at the poems that were written before the twentieth century. Do they deal with the same issues and topics? Do they treat them in the same way?

7   Look at the way poets from different times have used the sonnet form. Have any used it more effectively than others?

8   Look at how poets bring out aspects of the culture and tradition in which the poem is set. You could use:

    'Ain't I A Woman?' by Sojourner Truth (page 12)
    'Why Brownlee Left' by Paul Muldoon (page 13)
    'The Fear' by Robert Frost (page 16)
    'Baby-K Rap Rhyme' by Grace Nichols (page 56)
    'In Memory Of My Mother' by Patrick Kavanagh (page 66)
    'Night of the Scorpion' by Nissim Ezekiel (page 82)
    'My Uncle E. P. M. Harawa' by Felix Mnthali (page 84).

    You could also use the poems in the sections on:
    Seamus Heaney (page 118)
    Liz Lochhead (page 127)
    Grace Nichols (page 137).

Suggested Assignments

9   Explore how different poets treat the theme of losing someone very close to them. You could look at:

'My Grandmother' by Elizabeth Jennings (page 15)
'A Moment of Respect' by Edwin Brock (page 64)
'The Drawer' by George MacBeth (page 65)
'In Memory Of My Mother' by Patrick Kavanagh (page 66)
'For My Mother' by Elizabeth Jennings (page 67)
'On My First Son' by Ben Jonson (page 68).

10   Has the work of any one poet impressed you or given you particular enjoyment? Write a magazine article on that poet's work which expresses your pleasure. You may illustrate your article.

11   Imagine you are working for an advertising agency and you have to find specific poems, or extracts from poems, to help sell a product. Write an account of what you would propose. Describe the product, specify the texts you would use and explain why.

Writing on poetry in examinations

It is quite likely that at the end of an English or English Literature course you will be asked to write about poetry in an examination. Many people believe that it is quite inappropriate to be asked to respond sensitively to literature in such conditions, but it remains a common feature of many courses.

The range of texts you may have been asked to study is enormous – so is the range of questions which may be set. There are some general guidelines which may prove helpful, however.

Writing on prepared texts

◆ Be prepared for the examination. Study your set poetry carefully and know it well. Revise your texts before the examination and try to predict what sort of questions you might be asked.

◆ If you are allowed to use annotated texts during the examination this will help you, but don't rely upon the texts too much. Looking up references can be time-consuming.

◆ If you are not able to use texts in the examination, learn some short, useful extracts from the poetry that might support your writing.

◆ In the examination itself it is important to be well-organized and clear-thinking. Make sure you know which parts of the question paper you have to answer.

◆ Keep a careful check on time. Try to allocate your time accurately and avoid spending too much time on one part of the examination paper (most examination papers guide you on time allocation).

◆ Try to give yourself time to think and respond to the set questions and, if you have a choice, choose carefully.

◆ Spend a few minutes making *brief* notes before writing your response.

◆ If possible, look over what you have written and correct any errors before the examination ends.

Writing on unseen texts

Try not to be daunted by the examination conditions. Writing on an unseen text is much the same as writing in response to a single poem. Approach the poem as you would normally and think before you begin writing.

The notes on writing about a single poem on page 145 will help you.

Exam practice questions

Now look at these questions and attempt to answer them in timed conditions (no more than 60 minutes per question).

1 How has your study of Owen's poetry helped you to imagine what life was like for soldiers in World War 1? Refer to at least three poems.

2 Show how nature is described in any three of the poems in this book.

3 Explain how three poets in this book have recalled different aspects of childhood.

4 By referring to at least two poems, show that poetry can sometimes be very serious and sometimes quite amusing.

5 Choose two poems in which Wordsworth conveys strong feelings. Write about the way he conveys these feelings through the poems. You should comment on:

   ◆ the language he uses
   ◆ imagery and symbolism
   ◆ form.

6 Choose two poems written by Grace Nichols and explain those aspects of the poems which reveal that Grace Nichols is a poet writing from a black woman's point of view.

7 Look at 'Pike' by Ted Hughes and 'Revelation' by Liz Lochhead. What do the two poems have in common? Is it obvious that one is written by a male poet and the other by a female?

This poem should be used in conjunction with pages 34–35.

The Fight _____

I remember, when we were just nippers,
Michael Saunders and I were sworn foes;
One morning of sunlit September
It looked as though we'd come to blows

5 At playtime, quite close to the railings,
Out of sight from our teacher, Miss Bee,
I threatened that awful boy, Saunders,
And he in his turn threatened me.

He said that he'd tear me to ribbons.
10 'You and whose army?' I said.
(We were terribly witty in those days.)
I told him I'd kick in his head.

We circled each other, like panthers
(Out of range of each other, of course);
15 We glared at each other like tigers,
Observed by the greengrocer's horse.

A little crowd gathered around us;
They egged us both on to begin.
Kathy Woodward (who wetted her knickers)
20 Said she'd notify our next-of-kin.

Someone pushed me towards Michael Saunders;
Thank God, he stepped out of the way.
We started to take off our jackets . . .
A Spitfire, it was, saved the day.

25 Overhead, the Battle of Britain
Was beginning in earnest once more;
Like tigers and panthers, the aircraft
Were trying to settle the score.

They spat at each other with bullets;
30 When two of them fell in their flames
Miss Bee led us all to the shelters
To play mental arithmetic games.

Sometimes I see Michael Saunders
In the pub of a Saturday night.
35 Forty years have elapsed since that morning
When two little boys had a fight:

But Michael still often reminds me
Of that day. What he always says is:
'I bet you my Dad could beat your Dad,'
40 And I tell him that mine could beat his.

We play cards in the cosy bar-parlour,
Our glasses of beer side by side;
In the grate a brisk log-fire is burning;
We forget that it's winter outside

45 Where, in the adjacent graveyard,
Two pilots lie under the snow.
I wonder if Michael or I might have won:
But that's something that we'll never know.

Ted Walker

The following poem should be used in conjunction with pages 59–60.

Long Distance _____

Though my mother was already two years dead
Dad kept her slippers warming by the gas,
put hot water bottles her side of the bed
and still went to renew her transport pass.

5 You couldn't just drop in. You had to phone.
He'd put you off an hour to give him time
to clear away her things and look alone
as though his still raw love were such a crime.

He couldn't risk my blight of disbelief
10 though sure that very soon he'd hear her key
scrape in the rusted lock and end his grief.
He **knew** she'd just popped out to get the tea.

I believe life ends with death, and that is all.
You haven't both gone shopping; just the same,
15 in my new black leather phone book there's your name
and the disconnected number I still call.

Tony Harrison

The following poem should be used in conjunction with pages 7–8.

Death on a Live Wire

Treading a field I saw afar
A laughing fellow climbing the cage
That held the grinning tensions of wire,
Alone, and no girl gave him courage.

5 Up he climbed on the diamond struts.
Diamond cut diamond, till he stood
With the insulators brooding like owls
And all their live wisdom, if he would.

I called to him climbing and asked him to say
10 What thrust him into the singeing sky:
The one word he told me the wind took away,
So I shouted again, but the wind passed me by

And the gust of his answer tore at his coat
And struck him stark on the lightning's bough:
15 Humanity screeched in his manacled throat
And he cracked with flame like a figure of straw.

Turning, burning, he dangled black,
A hot sun swallowing at his fork
And shaking embers out of his back,
20 Planting his shadow of fear in the chalk.

O then he danced an incredible dance
With soot in his sockets, hanging at heels;
Uprooted mandrakes screamed in his loins,
His legs thrashed and lashed like electric eels;

25 For now he embraced the talent of iron,
The white-hot ore that comes from the hill,
The Word out of which the electrons run,
The snake in the rod and the miracle;

And as he embraced it the girders turned black,
30 Fused metal wept and great tears ran down,
Till his fingers like snails at last came unstuck
And he fell through the cage of the sun.

Michael Baldwin

Margin annotations (handwritten):

laughing, so he isn't scared

not sure about this bit?

was the poet there? He says so

he can't hear

gruesome language used

what are they?

ref. to the Bible. Why?

used again

falling down

very vivid

why a cage?

why a girl?

makes me think of birds on the wire

use of rhyme

like a tree

Why did he do it?

very vivid

unpleasant picture

creates a disturbing picture

funny description

it's a sad poem and quite vivid

lots of unpleasant pictures created

157

Glossary

Alliteration: the repetition of initial sounds in words next to or near each other (see page 22).

Ballad: a narrative poem which tells a dramatic story. Originally they were sung and many still exist as folk-songs (see page 38).

Couplet: a pair of rhyming lines (see page 44).

Elegy: a poem written as a lament for the death of someone, or written to record a passing event (see page 38).

Epitaph: a verse written to record, or celebrate, a person's life after they have died (see page 50).

Form: the way a poem is organized, its verse structure and rhyme scheme (see page 32).

Free verse: poetry which has no clearly-defined verse pattern or rhyme scheme (see page 38).

Imagery: the use of descriptive language to create an imagined picture or feeling for the reader (see page 21).

Metaphor: the presenting of one object in terms of another. A metaphor is a special kind of image which describes something as though it were something else. For example: 'the girl swam against the crowds to reach the bus' (see page 25). **Extended metaphor**: see pages 27–29.

Metre: the regular beat or rhythm used in a poem (see page 58).

Mood: the atmosphere created in a poem by careful use of vocabulary and word sounds. For example: sad, joyful, anxious and so on (see page 11). See also **Tone**.

Onomatopoeia: the use of words which imitate the actual sound of things. For example: clang, crash, slither and so on (see page 22).

Pace: the speed at which a poem needs to be read (see page 11).

Personification: the technique of referring to an animal or an object as if it were human and endowing it with human characteristics (see page 30).

Quatrain: a stanza or verse of four rhyming lines (see pages 44, 59).

Rhyme: words that have a matching sound quality and that sound alike (see page 52).

Rhyme scheme: the pattern in which rhyming sounds occur in a poem (see page 53).

Rhythm: the regular pattern of stressed and unstressed syllables (i.e. the 'beat') of a poem (see page 54). See also **Metre**.

Simile: the direct comparison of one thing with another, usually employing 'like' or 'as'. For example: 'it sank like a stone', 'it was as light as a feather' (see page 25).

Sonnet: a rhyming poem of fourteen lines (see page 44). **Sonnet sequence**: see page 44.

Stanza: a group of lines into which poems are often divided, forming a distinct visual unit (see page 38).

Structure: the internal organization of a poem, and the way in which the content is presented (see page 34).

Symbol: a particular kind of sign where the object represents not itself but other qualities. For example: a red rose could represent England or peace.

Theme: the main concern of a poem, the issues the poem addresses.

Tone: the attitude suggested by the voice of the poem. For example: sarcastic, gentle, mocking and so on (see page 11). See also **Mood**.

Verse: see **Stanza**.

Index of Poets

Index of First Lines

Heinemann Educational Publishers
Halley Court, Jordan Hill, Oxford OX2 8EJ
A division of Reed Educational and Professional Publishing Ltd

OXFORD MADRID ATHENS FLORENCE
PRAGUE CHICAGO PORTSMOUTH NH (USA)
MEXICO CITY SÃO PAULO SINGAPORE
KUALA LUMPUR TOKYO MELBOURNE
AUCKLAND NAIROBI KAMPALA
IBADAN GABORONE JOHANNESBURG

First published 1996

2000 99 98 97
10 9 8 7 6 5 4 3 2

ISBN 0 435 14044 2

Designed and typeset by GRAF Design
Illustrated by Jane Bottomley
Cover design by Moondisks Ltd.
Cover painting 'Composition III' by Franz Marc. Bridgeman Art Library/K.E. Osthaus Museum, Hagen.
Printed and bound in Great Britain by Bath Press Ltd.

Acknowledgements

The author and Publishers should like to thank the following for permission to use copyright material:–

A.M. Heath & Company on behalf of Michael Baldwin for 'Death on a Live Wire' © Michael Baldwin, p7, 157; Mary Dorcey for 'First Love', p9; Faber and Faber Limited for 'Why Brownlee Left' by Paul Muldoon, p13; David Higham Associates on behalf of Elizabeth Jennings for 'My Grandmother', p15, 'Transformations', p48, 'For My Mother', p67, from *Collected Poems* published by Carcanet Press Limited; Random House UK Limited for 'The Fear' from *The Poetry of Robert Frost* edited by Edward Connery Lathem, p16; Faber and Faber Limited for 'Preludes' by T.S. Eliot from *Collected Poems 1909-1962*, p23; Phoebe Hesketh for 'Geriatric Ward', p26 and 'Heatwave', p61; Laurence Pollinger Limited on behalf of the Estate of Frieda Lawrence Ravagli for an extract from *Odour of Chrysanthemums* from *The Collected Short Stories of D.H. Lawrence*, p60, and 'Flat Suburbs, S.W. in the Morning' from *The Collected Poems of D.H. Lawrence*, p27; Faber and Faber Limited for 'Mushrooms' by Sylvia Plath from *Collected Poems*, p30; Papermac for 'The Voice' from *The Collected Poems of Thomas Hardy* (1981), p53; Faber and Faber Limited for 'Night Mail' from *The Collected Poems of W.H. Auden*, p55; Curtis Brown Group Limited on behalf of Grace Nichols for 'Baby-K Rap Rhyme' © Grace Nichols 1991, p56; Peters Fraser & Dunlop Limited on behalf of Roger McGough for '40-Love' from *After the Merrymaking* published by Jonathan Cape Ltd., p32, 'W.P.C. Marjorie Cox' from *Holiday on Death Row* published by Jonathan Cape Ltd., p70, and 'Poem about the sun slinking off and pinning up a notice' from *Watchwords* published by Jonathan Cape Ltd., p33; Sheil Land Associates on behalf of Ted Walker for 'The Fight', p34, 155; Seán Sweeney, Trustee on behalf of the Estate of James Joyce for an extract from 'The Dead' in *Dubliners*, © Estate of James Joyce, p60; James Berry for 'Coming of the Sun', p61; Sheil Land Associates on behalf of the Estate of George MacBeth for 'The Drawer' © 1958, p65; Peter Fallon Literary Agent on behalf of the Estate of Patrick Kavanagh for 'In Memory of My Mother', p66; Wes Magee for 'Big Aunt Flo' from *Morning Break and Other Poems* by Wes Magee published by Cambridge University Press (1989) copyright © Wes Magee, p69; Dorothy Nimmo for 'A Woman's Work', p72; Little, Brown and Company (UK) for 'Woman Work' from *And Still I Rise* by Maya Angelou published by Virago Press, p73; Hodder Headline PLC for 'Daily London Recipe' by Steve Turner, p77; © Miroslav Holub for 'The Fly', p78; Oxford University Press for 'Vergissmeinnicht' from *The Complete Poems of Keith Douglas* edited by Desmond Graham (1978) copyright © Marie J. Douglas 1978, p80; Oxford University Press, New Delhi, for 'Night of the Scorpion' by Nissim Ezekiel, p82; Faber and Faber Limited for 'Pike' from *Lupercal*, p84, 155; 'Harvest Moon' from *Season Songs* by Ted Hughes, p112; 'February 17th' from *Moortown Diary* by Ted Hughes, p114; 'Hill-Stone was Content' from *Remains of Elmet* by Ted Hughes, p116; 'Honeymoon Flight' from *Death of a Naturalist* by Seamus Heaney, p119; 'A Constable Calls' from 'Singing School' in *North* by Seamus Heaney, p120; 'The Grauballe Man' from *North* by Seamus Heaney, p122; 'Sonnet No. 3' from 'Clearances' in *The Haw Lantern* by Seamus Heaney, p124; Polygon for 'Man on a Bench', p128, 'Revelation', p128 and 'Everybody's Mother', p130, from *Dreaming Frankenstein* by Liz Lochhead (1984); 'What-I'm-Not Song' (The Complete Alternative History of the World), p132, and 'Man Monologue No.5', p135, from *True Confessions* by Liz Lochhead (1985); Little, Brown and Company (UK) for 'Beauty', p138, 'Holding My Beads', p139, 'Praise Song for My Mother', p142, from *Fat Black Woman's Poems* by Grace Nichols published by Virago Press; 'Beverley's Saga', p140, and 'On Her Way to Recovery', p143, from *Lazy Thoughts of a Lazy Woman* by Grace Nichols published by Virago Press; Gordon Dickerson on behalf of Tony Harrison for 'Long Distance', p60, 156.

The Publishers have made every effort to trace the copyright holders, but if they have inadvertently overlooked any, they will be pleased to make the necessary arrangements at the first opportunity.

The Publishers should like to thank the following for permission to reproduce photographs on the pages noted:–

Neil Cooper/Panos Pictures, p12; B&C Alexander/Still Pictures, p22; ARDEA London Ltd, p28; Topham Picture Library, p37; The National Gallery p45; Nordic Summer Evening, 1899-1900 by Sven Richard Bergh (1858-1919) Goteborgs Konstmuseum, Sweden/Bridgeman Art Library, London, p48; The Hulton Getty Picture Collection Ltd, Unique House, p21-31 Woodfield Road London W9 2BA, p53; Environmental Picture Library/Pierre Gleizes, p56T; Panos Pictures/D. Sansoni, p56M1; Heidi Bradner/Panos Pictures, p56M2; Nick Robinson Panos Pictures, p56B; The Bridgeman Art Library, p68; Kings College, Cambridge, p76; Peter Newark's Military Pictures, p80; Mansell Collection, p87; NHPA © David Woodfall, p89; Christina Rossetti by Dante Gabriel Rossetti (1828-82) Fitzwilliam Museum, University of Cambridge/Bridgeman Art Library, London, p94; © British Musem, p96; Nativity, Bedford Hours, French, (c.1423) British Library, London/Bridgeman Art Library, London, p99; Chatto & Windus. The Hogarth Press, p101; Imperial War Museum, p104; Imperial War Museum, p107; Faber and Faber Publishers © Niall McDiarmid, p109; Ace Photo Agency, p113; Collections/Fay Godwin, p116; Faber and Faber Publishers © Caroline Forbes, p118; © Skyscan Balloon Photography, p119; Topham Picture Source, p122; The Ulster Museum, p125; Penguin Books, p127; Pantechnicon, p134; Virago, p137; J. Allan Cash Ltd, p138; Portrait of a Lady, c. 1455 by Roger van der Weyden, (1399-1464) National Gallery of Art, Washington DC/Bridgeman Art Library, London, p139; Betty Press/Panos Pictures, p142; © Martin Mayer Network Photographers, p154.